HIS STORY IN ITALY

Lyn and Dorothy,
It is great to be a
part of God's family.
Yours for Christ in Italy,

Fred Whitman

Fred Whitman

Prov. 3:5,6

Perugia, Italy

MMXI

To Rachel,

My bride,

My wise help-meet,

The tireless mother of my children

And keeper of our home

As well as my first love,

According to the will of God

Who by His Grace chose us,

Redeemed us,

Called us,

Enabled us,

Sent us out,

Provided for us

And encouraged us

To serve Him all these years

Together.

PREFACE

Having well passed my 60th birthday (if I was Moses, I would have just become middle-aged), I have finally decided to write down, before my memory is all gone, the story of what God did to get me to Italy and what He has been doing in Italy from the perspective of the Whitman family—HIS STORY in Italy.

This year is the fiftieth anniversary of the March Missions Conference at Faith Bible Church in Carlisle, New York, when the Lord called me to give my life up for Him, to lay it on the altar of foreign missions. I was twelve years old. It has been no sacrifice. The Lord has blessed my life so much and in so many ways that it will be difficult to limit the size of this book.

It is humbling to be at this point in our ministry and feel that we are just getting started, but we know that our times are not the Lord's times. In fact, one of His days is like a thousand of our years, so we'll just keep pressing on and trusting him for the next sunset and sunrise.

As you read this account of HIS STORY in Italy, I trust that your heart will swell with thanksgiving to the One who works all things according to His will and purpose. To Him be the glory forever. Amen!

Yours for Christ in Italy,

Fred Whitman   February 26, 2011

UNFOLDING HIS STORY

CHAPTER ONE

It Is Great to Be a Part of a Family!
1612

After considerable Bible study and much contact with the non-conformists of early seventeenth-century England, Litchfield's resident tailor, Edward Wightman came to believe in and base his life upon Biblical principles. He became notorious for his Anabaptist views through his utterances made at the meetings of the Puritan Divines held in his district. He and his wife decided not to baptize their children. This unpopular position brought him into disfavor with the local religious authorities. The ink on the new 1611 King James Bible wasn't dry before Wightman was summoned to appear before King James I to answer for the accusations of heresy brought against him. His trial lasted for "sundry days," and on December 14, 1611, his sentence was pronounced in the Cathedral of Litchfield. The writ for his execution is dated March 9, 1612, and was directed to the Sheriff of Litchfield who had Edward Wightman brought to the stake.

Dawn came much too swiftly on Saturday, March 29, 1612. Edward was escorted to the Litchfield Market Square by local political and religious authorities, tied to the stake, and the fire was ignited. In that moment of crisis, perhaps it was the heat of the flames, or perhaps it was the tears of his wife—soon to become a young widow with five small children, one only a few months old—but the fact remains that he screamed to his murderers to have mercy and they pulled him out of the flames.

The authorities promptly threw him back into solitary confinement in the prison where he would remain for two weeks. During those difficult days, the communications that he received from his wife urged him to remain firm in his faith and not to deny his Lord.

On April 12, 1612, the Saturday between Good Friday and Easter, Edward was pulled out of his prison cell and brought to Market Square where he was to sign a document publicly renouncing his non-conformist, separatist faith and expressing his intention to return to the Anglican Church. As his wife cried out to him not to deny his Lord, he was brought in chains before the magistrate and the official renouncement which he was to sign was placed before him.

To the surprise of his persecutors, he refused to renounce his faith and sign the papers. Edward was immediately taken and tied to a pole. Kindling wood was piled around him. The flame was ignited, and while listening to the pleas of his wife to remain stalwart in his faith, this courageous man of God gave his life in martyrdom.

AN ARTIST'S IMPRESSION OF THE SCENE IN MARKET SQUARE
WHEN EDWARD WIGHTMAN WAS BURNED AT THE STAKE

It is my privilege and responsibility to be a twelfth-generation descendent of Edward Wightman, the last "heretic" to die by burning in England.

It was also my privilege in 1996 to visit Litchfield, England, and to find the place in Market Square where this martyrdom took place.

The event is now remembered by a plaque on the outside wall of the old Catholic-turned-Anglican Church, now a community center.

EDWARD WIGHTMAN
OF BURTON-ON-TRENT
WAS BURNT AT THE STAKE
IN THIS MARKET PLACE
FOR HERESY
11TH APRIL 1612
BEING THE LAST PERSON
IN ENGLAND SO TO DIE.

Edward's children immigrated to the colony of Connecticut in the new world. Valentine was the founding pastor of the First Baptist Church of Groton in 1705 and remained its pastor for forty-two years before being succeeded as pastor by his son Timothy who then pastored the church for forty years. In 1724, Rev. Valentine along with his brother, Rev. Daniel Wightman, led in the formation of the First Baptist Church of New York City. On May 20, 1725, while pastoring the First Baptist Church of Groton, Connecticut, he wrote a letter "To the Elders and Brethren of the Baptised Churches in Rhode Island" which he began with these words:

"I am under some concern to write a plea for a neglected ordinance, to whit, that of singing psalms, hymns or spiritual songs. And therefore in order thereunto, I shall, God assisting, First prove singing of psalms, hymns, or spiritual songs to be the duty of Gentile believers under the Gospel. Secondly, that is a moral duty. Thirdly, what singing is. Fourthly, how it ought to be performed."
(Wightman, Wade C. *The Wightman Ancestry.* Chelsea, MI: Bookcrafters, 1997. 1789-1791.)

Wightman wrote this treatise on singing as a part of public worship and introduced this innovation to his services, but the practice was met with scant support by those of his time.

CHAPTER TWO

Great-Grandpa Cook –
An Adopted Missionary Heritage in Brazil
1900

In the late 1890s, Rev. William Ayes Cook felt the call of God to take the Gospel to the unreached indigenes in unexplored areas of Brazil. He traveled by steamer to Rio de Janeiro, then by train to São Paulo, Ribeirão Preito, and Uberaba. At this point, he traveled north by horse, canoe, and raft to a land where few had ever been before with the Gospel.

On several occasions, as he distributed Gospel literature, there were attempts on his life due to the instigation of the religious powers that had held Brazil and most of the continent of South America in their grip for nearly four hundred years.

(Rev. Cook's camp site)

In primitive and life-challenging situations, Grandpa Cook forced his way through the underbrush, across the rivers, and through many dangerous rapids to take Scripture portions to people who had never heard of the death Christ died to redeem them from their sins.

The driving force that consumed his soul and gave him the strength to forge ahead over nearly 10,000 miles of formerly uncharted territory in the heart of Brazil is best expressed by the last chapter of his book Through the Wilderness of Brazil by Horse, Canoe and Float:

INCONCEIVABLE TREASURES SQUANDERED –
CHRISTIAN EXPANSION

In addition to one hundred thousand or more human victims, the annual money offering to Saint Bacchus in the United States averages sixteen dollars per capita for the entire population, and an additional tax of twelve dollars per capita because of crime. Ten dollars per capita more is consumed annually in the terrible vice of gambling; eight dollars for tobacco; five dollars for theatres; one dollar sixty for candy, and fifty cents for chewing gum. In contrast to this, only about eleven cents per capita is given as a nation, or thirty-five cents for each church member, to Christian foreign Missions.

In other words, this Christian nation gives six times as much for chewing gum. Thirty times as much for automobiles, seventeen times as much for candy, fifty-five times as much for theatres, eighty-eight times as much for tobacco, one hundred eleven times as much for gambling, and three hundred thirty-three times as much to sustain the worship of Saint Bacchus and to care for his worshippers as it gives to extend the glorious reign of the Prince of Peace in lands beyond our own. Our national contribution each year to Saint Bacchus would give a house and lot costing three thousand dollars to eight hundred thousand families—would build annually a Chicago or a Philadelphia. Surely, in view of our stupendous offerings to luxury and vice, we are able to increase enormously our benevolence. If each church member should give the value of a letter postage each week, it would increase the offering to foreign missions threefold...

Selfishness or the self-centered life cannot comprehend giving time, or substance or self to the service of Christ. It can understand trading only. It needs nothing less than the Spirit of Heaven in Christ's disciples to free them from the low, sordid spirit and principles of the age.

But what God requires of you, dear reader, is not merely your substance, but rather and supremely, YOURSELF and YOUR LOVE. Jesus longs to reproduce Himself in each one of His followers. How exalted a life it is to live to reproduce Christ! The watchword of the church should be always, "Every believer like Christ, first, most and always, a soul winner." TO GATHER INTO CHRIST THE SOULS HE DIED TO SAVE, IS THE SUPREME OBJECT FOR WHICH THE CHURCH EXISTS," and "TO WIN FOR THE LAMB THAT WAS SLAIN THE REWARD OF HIS SUFFERINGS."

Can one be a true disciple of Jesus and not believe in the divine enterprise of Foreign Missions? When you pray, "Thy will be done on earth as it is in Heaven," is this not a solemn petition that the LAW of Heaven may become the law of the whole earth and of ALL mankind? Does not "God so loved the world that He gave his one Son," mean that God loved and gave his Son for ALL mankind of whatever race or social condition—for the most degraded savage no less than for the most exalted civilized man? Does not, "Man shall not live by bread alone but by every word of God," mean all men? ...

The Lord Jesus Christ, the great missionary, abdicating the Eternal Throne, renounced the supreme majesty of Deity to become a poor, despised foreign missionary in a world overflowing with all manner of evil and misery, that He might redeem, transform and transfigure, physically, mentally, spiritually and socially the most unworthy and the most unfit. "He saved others, Himself He could not save." "He saw the travail of His soul and was satisfied." He was not advertised as a "great preacher" in receipt of a "big salary." He "was despised and rejected" by the "great." He did not preach in a palatial "First Church" with a ten-thousand-dollar organ and four or five-thousand-dollar choir behind him, and a millionaire congregation before him; nor did He hide himself away in His "Study" from the needy world. His auditorium was the star-adorned universe; His pulpit, the fishermen's boat, the hillside and the highway, the moneyless man's cottage and the "moneyed" man's residence; His congregation, the "masses," His music, the spontaneous and triumphant songs of the redeemed, whose hearts were bursting with gladness and thanksgiving; His recompense, transformed men. May not Christ's disciples of the present day follow Him, when needful, in His methods of evangelizing and mode of life? ...

There was never such an age of opportunity for the Church as NOW. What a supreme happiness it is to be the instrument whereby a degraded, brutalized, human soul is implanted with the divine life, and is made to germinate, blossom, and grow beautiful and fragrant as the rose of Sharon by the life-imbuing breath of the son of God! It surpasses in sweetness all other human experience; it is an age-enduring benediction. To relieve disease of soul and mind is the highest and holiest function possible to man.

Dear reader, you have kindly and patiently followed me through this volume. I trust that you know from personal experience, the nobility, the exaltation, the exquisite pleasure and happiness of such a life. If you have found Him a mighty Savior, and need Him every hour, and He fills your soul with gladness, do not our neighbors of the great southern continent need Him also?

"Our desire for you is that ye might be filled with the knowledge of His will in all wisdom and spiritual understanding; that ye might walk worthy of the Lord unto all pleasing, bearing fruit in every good work, and increasing in the knowledge of God."

(Cook, William A. *Through the Wilderness of Brazil By Horse, Canoe and Float.* New York: American Tract Society, 1909. 484-485.)

Rev. Cook penned these words in Wellsville, New York, where he lived in a boardinghouse in the months after returning to the United States after his time in Brazil. The boardinghouse was run by Ella Belle Pierce who had been left a widow after the home-going of her husband, my natural great-grandfather, Millard Fillmore Pierce. In 1912, Rev. Cook married my widowed great-grandmother, and they lived for two years in their home on Broad Street in Wellsville, New York, before moving west.

Grandpa Cook held pastorates in South Dakota, Minnesota, Iowa, and Illinois. He went to be with the Lord on February 26, 1932.

CHAPTER THREE

God Brought Me into This World,
He Will also Take Care of Me
1948-1950

One hot July Wednesday, there was excitement in the home of young Pastor George and Jean Whitman. God would soon bless their parsonage with a little baby, their first. They didn't know how they would pay for this bundle of joy on their $15-a-week salary, but they were confident that God would meet the need. The French were celebrating their Independence Day on July 14th, and the church was gathered for its Wednesday evening Bible study and prayer time, led by the deacons, when the doctor informed the 22-year-old pastor and his 19-year-old wife that they had been blessed with a baby boy, scrawny as he was at 5 lbs. 3 oz. stretched over a 21-inch frame. His name would be Frederick Lavern, in honor of his two grandfathers. With joy in his heart, Pastor George left his wife and firstborn to go share the news with the church family and begin to prepare for his Sunday services at the Carmel Baptist Church in Mosiertown, Pennsylvania.

In between that Sunday's services, the pastor spent considerable time on his knees in prayer in the privacy of the parsonage. At the same time as he thanked the Lord for this blessing in their lives, he was pleading with Him to show His power in providing the money with which to pay the hospital bill as well as the doctor's delivery fee. On Monday, he was to bring baby and mother home, and he had no money with which to pay the bills!

After the Sunday evening service, the pastor was preparing to close up the church when one of the young people called him outside because one of the men of the church wanted to speak with him. This faithful church member wanted to apologize for missing the evening service. His cows had broken down the fence, and he had spent the evening repairing the fence and chasing them back onto his property. But that wasn't the real reason why he had called for the pastor. He had recently sold two cows, and he and his wife had decided to give a part of the proceeds to their pastor to help him pay his doctor bills at this time. With some embarrassment, he stuffed several bills into the pastor's suit-coat pocket. He then said goodbye to the pastor and went on his way.

Pastor Whitman went back inside the church to continue closing up the church. He stopped on the steps leading up into the auditorium and anxiously pulled the bills out of his pocket. He counted: one, two, three, four, five, six, seven, eight, nine, ten. There were ten ten-dollar bills! He had no sooner placed them in his wallet than he was greeted by the president of the church's youth group who handed him an envelope containing $20. His heart cried out to God in thanksgiving! He had started out the day without a possibility of bringing his wife and new baby home from the hospital, but in the course of the day, he had been given his weekly salary of $15 as well as two cash gifts totaling $120! He couldn't wait for morning to come so that he could rush to the hospital and share the good news with Jean.

Bright and early the next morning, Pastor Whitman was at the hospital to pay with cash his $85 bill. After mother and baby were discharged, they decided to stop by the doctor's office to pay something on his bill for the prenatal visits and delivery. The doctor's secretary was quite flustered as she could not find any record of the doctor's services, so as soon as he was finished with a patient, she called him out of his office. He took the ledger, slowly looked through it, and said, "There is nothing written here. It looks like this one is on me! There will be no charge for my services!" With this good news, the new parents were able to stop on their way home and buy a crib for baby Freddie.

Frederick LaVern Whitman—
8 mos. old

Being a P.K. (Preacher's Kid), I had a constant exposure from the earliest days to missionaries in our home. I was just learning my first words when a missionary to India taught me to say "Bat-ti'," the Indian word for light. Some thirty-two years later, without realizing that it was one of the first words that I had pronounced, I chose this word in another language as the name for the Italian Christian radio station that I helped to found—"Radio Luce" (Radio Light). In those early years as I would play by myself, probably following the example of my preacher dad, I was often heard shouting the words, "Bible me!"

At Nasons – Near Edinbur

CHAPTER FOUR

Early Awakenings to God's Grace
1953-1955

In the fall of 1953, there were evangelistic meetings with Dr. Merle Fuller at the First Baptist Church of Edinboro, Pennsylvania, where Pastor Whitman was pastoring. One evening after the service, as my mom was praying with my sister Lois and me before putting us to bed as she always did, she asked us if we had understood anything from the message. I replied that I had understood that Jesus had died for me on the cross and that I needed to accept Him into my life as my own personal Savior. Lois responded in the same way, so both of us got out of our beds, knelt down, and prayed, asking Jesus to forgive us of our sins, inviting Him to come into our lives as our personal Savior. He did! Although I was only five years old and Lois was only four, we both understood that night our need of the Lord Jesus and put our trust in Him. By God's grace, that night we passed from death into life and entered the family of God! That night we passed over the bridge of the cross into God's eternal forgiveness and new life in Christ from which there is no return.

During those formative years, Lois and I were already preparing for future service, singing duets in two-part harmony on our dad's weekly radio program in Meadville, Pennsylvania. Serving God as a family was the mentality in which we were raised, and even though we had to stand on chairs to reach the microphone we were going to do it. There was one chorus, however, that we did not like to sing, but our father insisted that we sing it for the glory of God whether we wanted to or not. The words went like this:

"Over in glory we'll not shed a tear,
No disappointment, no heart-ache, no tears,
Singing and shouting, glad praises, oh so grand,
Living forever in the Glory land."

Many were the times that we sang it through sobs and a river of tears thinking of the spanking that we would receive if we didn't do it.

In March of 1952, Dad took Mom to the hospital and later came home to announce to Lois and me that we had a new baby brother, Duane. My response was, "We have too much kids."

FRED
LOIS
DUANE

Over the next years, the Lord added Rebecca, James, Dorcas, and Dwight to the Whitman parsonage, and I am thankful for each one of them!

One evening that I well remember was one at the supper table in the parsonage at Edinboro when a loud boom was followed by the entire kitchen cupboard crashing to the floor with all of its contents. A car being driven by a drunken man had not negotiated the "Y" in the road. It had slammed directly into our house that was built between the two roads that joined at the intersection.

I also recall a cold November evening when my dad came back from a successful hunting trip in the Pennsylvania mountains. The deer carcass had frozen solid on the roof of the car during the trip home, and when dad came in the door as a triumphant hunter, he brought in the deer as well, standing it up in the living room! That made quite an impression on us kids... however, much less on our mom I am sure.

In 1955, God's call came to Pastor Whitman to move the family from the First Baptist Church in Edinboro, a college town in northwestern Pennsylvania, to Faith Bible Church, a small church built on the corner of a cornfield two miles outside of Carlisle, New York, a town of about 300 inhabitants. The parsonage was the farmhouse of one of the members of the church. Moving from a parsonage built in the "Y" of a major street leading into the town of Edinboro to a farmhouse on a dirt road in the country where cars seldom even drove by was quite an experience. For months, it was very difficult to sleep at night because of the absolute peace and quiet of our new home. Our landlord was very patient with us children as we were introduced to the rigors of farm life. We never got over the excitement of going in the barn to help with chores or of seeing white-tail deer coming near the house. We did eventually get used to the smell of the barnyard.

One of the priceless experiences provided us two older Whitman children was attendance in a one-room schoolhouse in Carlisle, New York, for our first and second grades. It is difficult to understand how Mrs. Hazard kept track of all of those kids while teaching them their subjects, but she did. In fact, I had a first-hand experience in this regard that the Lord used to teach me a valuable lesson for my life.

Being one of four children at that time meant that there wasn't a lot of extra money for store-bought treats. My daily bag lunch consisted of a bologna sandwich, some fruit, and possibly some homemade cookies. One day, I eyed a delicious-looking candy bar that Peter Schuppel, the boy at the neighboring desk, pulled out of his lunch box. He left his lunch on the desk to go to the bathroom, and in an instant, that candy bar was unwrapped and in my mouth. It wasn't nearly as good as I had expected, especially when I had to lie to my friend and deny having seen it.

The school day ended, and finally it was time to go home. Pastor Whitman picked up his two children and took them home. On the way in the car, he quizzed me regarding my day and especially how I had enjoyed my lunch. It soon came out that Mrs. Hazard had seen the candy robbery; but instead of making a public spectacle, embarrassing the preacher's son in front of the entire class, she had called the pastor. Upon arrival at the house, indeed my Dad dealt with the situation. A spanking was in order, but it didn't stop there. After the tears were dried and the sobs quieted, this little second-grade thief was sent to get what money I might have had in my savings bank, and two candy bars would be bought to replace the one that had been stolen. The trip to the store was difficult, but the trip to the friend's house was worse. This disobedient child had to ring the doorbell, explain what had happened to the mother of my friend, and then call Peter and give him the candy bars to replace the stolen one. A valuable lesson in honesty was learned that day. God sees everything but sometimes he uses the authority figures in our life to make us aware of it.

CHAPTER FIVE

A Privileged Preacher's Kid
1956

At a certain point, as the Word of God was faithfully preached, I became aware that my walk of obedience to the Lord would not go forward until I followed my Savior in believer's baptism by immersion. The Faith Bible Church at Carlisle, which was pastored by my dad at this time, did not have a baptistery, so as people would trust Christ as Savior and Lord and would express the desire to be baptized, the church would use the facilities of the Fort Plain Baptist Church about 15 miles away. After a doctrinal interview by the pastor (my dad) and deacons, Lois, several others and I who had recently been saved were baptized. It was a joyous experience which I still remember very clearly.

In third grade, my class put on a circus, and I was asked by the teachers to be the Master of Ceremonies. That was a rewarding experience as, for the first time, this future preacher-missionary had the responsibility of standing up in front of a group and leading a program. It sure beat being a clown or an elephant!

That summer was my first opportunity to attend a Christian camp. It was also the first time that I had to stay overnight for several days away from my parents. In addition to quietly crying myself to sleep, one memory of this experience bears repeating. In addition to paying for the week at camp, my parents were able to give me one dollar so that I could buy a coke or have an ice cream bar each day. Each cost only a dime! The first day at camp, it was so exciting to visit the craft shack that I bought a small address book for each of my parents, totaling eighty cents. That left me with twenty cents for the week to spend on myself. It also taught me a valuable lesson: the joy of giving. Doing something for my parents was far more rewarding than eating an ice cream at the snack shack.

That winter, we had a blizzard that seemed to last forever. For several weeks, the school was closed. When it was reopened, we had to walk home for over a mile from the closest place that the bus could arrive to our house. One situation sticks in my mind. Since we had to walk home each evening, we would not arrive in time for our favorite cartoons. One evening, I ran ahead of my little sister in order to arrive home in time to watch the program. I was not thinking of how my parents would react to me getting home in the middle of a snowstorm without Lois. After my dad walked back down the road to find Lois and bring her back to the house, I received the spanking of a lifetime (one of many). I never did that again.

CHAPTER SIX

Study Music to Someday Use It for God
1958-1965

In fifth grade, I had the privilege of beginning music lessons at the Cobleskill Central School. It was decided that Freddie would study violin and Lois the viola. Since both Pastor and Mrs. Whitman were musical and the two children had already demonstrated the ability to sing, it seemed to be a good choice to study a stringed instrument to further develop their musical ear. Hours of practice led to later participation in the school orchestra, the all-county orchestra, and many other valuable learning experiences. Less fortunate were my three attempts to study the piano from Mom Whitman. The piano lessons came to a halt each time I had to try and play with two hands.

After my sixth grade, the Whitman family moved from the farmhouse on Bear Swamp Road to the new parsonage that had been built on the Carlisle-Canajoharie Road right next door to the church. The construction of our new home had been led by my grandfather, G. Frederick Whitman, who had worked as a carpenter for many years. I remember helping to carry the cement blocks. It was nice to give a hand to my grandpa, my dad, and the other men.

As nice as it was to move into a new house, it meant moving to a new school district. Consequently, we children all had to make what seemed to be an infinite number of new friendships. It seemed at the time like a tragedy, but the Lord used it to be a wonderful blessing in our lives. After the first week of classes, I was taken from the classroom where I had already made many new friends and was moved to the advanced section. It was scary to begin all over making acquaintances. However, one boy immediately befriended me and made me feel liked and wanted. Bob Frank has been a wonderful friend through thick and thin ever since.

The new school, Canajoharie Central School, had a wonderful music program. As I began my seventh grade, my violin lessons had progressed to the point that I was able to join the orchestra directed by Mrs. Judith (Judy) McMillian. Since I also wanted to play in the band, I began trumpet lessons and soon was proficient enough to join the band directed by Mr. William (Stan) McMillian. I also joined the boys' chorus directed by Miss Mary R. Shimer.

(Stan and Judy McMillian in Assisi)

After eight lessons on the trumpet and several Sundays of practicing songs out of the hymnbook while waiting for my mom to fix Sunday dinner, my dad insisted that I play a special number in the Sunday evening service. The easiest hymn that I found was "Great is Thy Faithfulness," so I played that one, never dreaming how many times the truth of God's faithfulness would prove itself anew in my life of service for the Savior.

Each musical experience was very important in the life of this young preacher's kid, but perhaps the greatest achievements were reached in the vocal field with my selection for the All State Chorus for the State of New York in my final two years of high school. Having never seen the inside of a luxury hotel like the one at Kiamisha Lake in the Catskills or the historic one in downtown Buffalo, I was a little confused with what to do with all the silverware that I found at the table each meal, being used to sitting at a crowded kitchen table with six other siblings and my parents. It was exciting to be chosen as one of four soloists in a spiritual for the final concert of the All State Convention in 1966, but the frightful experience of finding myself on stage before several thousand people made it difficult for me to get a note out. Thankfully, the others carried on with the song and we were all greeted with a great applause. I never asked the other three if they were aware that I wasn't singing, just mouthing the words.

In high school, it was a challenge to leave home Monday mornings with a violin (I later switched to a string bass), a trumpet, a book bag, and a gym bag. It was sometimes difficult to coordinate music and sports activities. However, in the four years of being part of the wrestling team, only once did it really create a problem.

Throughout high school, I was on the wrestling team, as a freshman and sophomore wrestling in the 95 lb. class and then as a junior and senior in the 103 lb. class. During my senior year of high school, the team was undefeated except for one dual match. That match came during the week that I was participating at the All State Chorus Festival at Kiamisha Lake in the Catskills. In my absence, our wrestling team lost a meet by exactly the points lost by the younger wrestler who took my place. That was hard to live down with Coach Colavito and the rest of the team. We missed out on an undefeated year because of my music festival!

CHAPTER SEVEN

The Choice Between Being a Missionary or a Mission-Field 1960

When I was twelve years of age, I felt the call of God to give my life for missions at the close of a service during a missions conference at Faith Bible Church where my dad was ministering. The main speaker was missionary Roy "Chick" Watkins, who had served the Lord for many years in Liberia, West Africa. As the Word was preached, I realized that I could not live my life for any reason other than giving it to the Lord's service in taking the Gospel to those who have never heard.

As we discussed the important subject of discerning the Lord's will for our lives, a very powerful illustration was given. The image was given of a ship in harbor whose rudder could be turned at will without effecting any change whatsoever in the direction of the ship. Once that ship began moving out to sea, however, the slightest movement of the rudder would quickly change its direction. I saw the need to start moving my life for God in the direction of missions, trusting Him to change the direction of my rudder as He would see fit. I was not going to spend my life saying "I am willing" when what I needed to do was step out by faith, start moving, and trust the Lord to lead me to that place of service for His glory.

When the invitation was given, I was the first one to the front. I was going to organize my life in a way that I could serve the Lord in Liberia, trusting Him to lead me in that direction and close the doors and open them according to His plan for me. I believe that there were others that night, too, at the missions conference at Faith Bible Church of Carlisle, New York, who gave their life to the Lord for missionary service. Among them was Janet Hunt who has served the Lord for many years in Japan.

As I look back on that night, I am filled with wonder and thanksgiving to the One who chose me by His Grace before the foundations of the world. Today, as I come in contact with children who express interest in serving the Lord as a missionary, I wonder how many of them will have a family like I did who will encourage them in following God's will for their life regardless of the cost.

I chose for my life verse Proverbs 3:5-6: "Trust in the Lord with all thine heart, lean not unto thine own understanding. In all thy ways acknowledge Him and He shall direct thy paths."

God's call in my life was reinforced each year at our church's annual mission conference, as well as at the weeks of summer camp I attended at BaYouCa (Baptist Youth Camp) in Smithville Flatts, New York. I was also enrolled for five years in the Bible Memory Association's youth memory program which gave me the opportunity each summer of attending Miracle Camp in Amsterdam, New York. The Lord used this experience as well to provide for spiritual growth in my life. Over the years it was a special blessing for me to be invited back to those camps as the missionary speaker!

CHAPTER EIGHT

Scholarships – Medicine or Missions?
1966

As my high school graduation drew nearer, so did the choice of a school where I could prepare for missionary service. From my earliest memories, I had planned on going to my Dad's alma mater, the Practical Bible Training School in Binghamton, New York. On many occasions, we had attended their annual retreat and commencement services. There wasn't even a question in my mind about it. However, in my senior year, a couple of events put this decision in crisis.

At the Ames Bible Conference, an annual event which our church always participated in, there were frequently guest speakers and musicians from Baptist Bible Seminary in Johnson City, New York. That year, one of the speakers was Dr. G. Arthur Woolsey, president of the college, along with a men's trio composed of Doug Hill, Paul Gustine, and Larry Henderson. The messages from First John as well as the special music put a seed in my heart. Perhaps that school would be a good place to prepare to serve God with my life and hopefully to be a part of a musical group too!

In the same time period, I received notice that I had placed well in the New York State Regents Scholarship Exam and would most certainly be awarded a scholarship for the accredited college of my choice in New York State. Baptist Bible Seminary qualified as one of these. At that point, I began rethinking my plans. Not wanting to disappoint my dad who had graduated from Practical Bible Training School, I was hesitant to choose Baptist Bible, but since I would be receiving a large state scholarship by going there, 1 knew he would probably feel relieved. I am sure that he was wondering how, with a pastor's salary, he would support the family as well as help me in college.

My Christian guidance counselor, knowing that I planned on going to Africa as a missionary, offered me another opportunity. If I wanted to study medicine, I would receive a scholarship from the town of Canajoharie for at least the first four years of medical college as long as I would agree to come back to Canajoharie and practice medicine for four years after I finished my specialization. I decided that I really didn't want to spend another ten years in school as well as another four years working at home before I could head out to the mission field. I'll never know if I would have made a good doctor or not; however, I do have terrible handwriting!

At my graduation from the Canajoharie High School, I was notified of another scholarship through the school should I decide to go to an accredited college. How wonderfully God provided for my college education. Being the oldest of seven children, I was aware that my parents, on Dad's salary as a pastor, would not be able to help me financially. So God took care of my college bill so that my parents didn't have to deal with that pressure.

After graduation from high school, I was also able to work for the summer at the Franlands Farm near Cobleskill with the France Family, members of our church, helping them get in the hay and milk their large herd of cows as well as help them show their prize-winning cattle at the Schoharie County Fair in

Cobleskill, New York. With the whopping dollar-an-hour salary, I was able to put several hundred dollars away toward my college expenses.

CHAPTER NINE

Preparation to Serve –
Studies, Service, and Social Life
1966-1970

It was a sunny day in central New York when the Whitman family packed their oldest son, his boxes for college, and his six siblings in their Volkswagen van and headed down old Route 7 to Johnson City, New York. After registration and setting up my room, they left me there at Crocker Dorm with my new suite-mates and future friends for a lifetime, Paul T. Plew and John Poole. I never did know where they got the name Crocker Dorm except for the fact that it was on Crocker Ave. For us, it meant "crotchety," and it was certainly a fire trap. However, out of that humble setting in the fall of 1966 came several choice servants of the Lord: our resident assistants Joe Flatt and Tim Wilhite, Paul Plew, John Poole, Powers Patent, and Tom Mather, to name only a few.

There are not many memories of that time except for classes, my part-time job at the IBM plant in Endicott, endless dorm meetings, and a couple of times when my folks were able to come down from Carlisle, and later, New Berlin, New York, to visit me. It was especially appreciated when my mom brought me down a batch of her famous cream puffs, which had to be kept under lock and key in the dorm for obvious reasons.

Crocker Dorm was many blocks from the main campus, and on those sub-zero mornings, knowing that hot coffee and breakfast were waiting for me in the cafeteria, I learned how to walk very fast, a habit that I have kept until the present time. In fact, I know very few people who enjoy walking as fast as I do.

Those were exciting days as I learned how well my local church, my Sunday School classes, my youth group, and my Dad's preaching had taught me the Word of God and how to study it. There was a lot to learn, but I was better off than many. When I had committed my life to missions, I had begun reading my Bible through each year, and this made Old and New Testament Bible Survey with Dr. Jacobs a very enjoyable review.

Weekends were also very enjoyable as, thanks to my friendship with Paul Plew, I was frequently invited to his home at Hunts Corners (outside the metropolis of Marathon, New York). His mom and dad, Harlow and Dorothy, were a second set of parents for me. In this time period, I met the Sisson family at the Hunts Corners Baptist Church just up the road from the Plew residence. Many years later in the home office at Cleveland, I renewed acquaintances with Ronnie Sisson (Watters) who was in the medical department of Baptist Mid-Missions for many years.

Many other weekends of the school year, however, were filled with serving the Lord in various local churches in a Gospel team ministry as a men's quartet that had been formed with John Poole, Paul Plew, and John Greening. I remember one very special weekend that we ministered at Hunt's Corners

Baptist Church with our classmate, Ken Mosher, who shared from his heart and from the Word what God had done in his life. Ken, along with his wife Eleanor, remained at BBC where he was in the athletic department for many years.

During my freshman year, my roommate was John Poole, who has served the Lord for many years with his wife Donna in the pastorate in Michigan. For our sophomore year, we had to find our own housing, so Paul Plew, John Poole, and I found a little attic apartment near the hospital and very near the campus of Baptist Bible Seminary in Johnson City.

During the first week of our sophomore year, I was asked to join a musical group which became known as The Anchormen. We were a trumpet trio/men's quartet with Roger Killian as group leader, first trumpet, and bass, Chris Hindal as second trumpet and baritone, myself as third trumpet and first tenor, and Paul Plew as pianist and lead tenor. The Lord gave us the privilege of traveling together representing the Lord and BBC for three school years and part of four summers in literally hundreds of churches and camps and several GARBC National Conferences. This experience was one of the most valuable of my entire time in college. Not only did we travel alone, ministering in Word and song across the nation, but we had the opportunity of traveling often with Dr. Wendell Kempton who mentored us and remained very close to us until the Lord called him home in 2008.

FW. Chris, Roger, Paul

One experience of many remains in my thoughts. One very busy weekend, we were scheduled for a youth rally and a weekend ministry at the First Baptist Church of Hornell, New York. Dr. Kempton was not feeling well, so as we traveled from the school in Johnson City to Hornell, he gave us his sermon outline and divided it up so that each of us would preach a part of it for him. God blessed, and we had a great weekend for God's glory.

As we traveled in our Gospel team ministry, knowing that I would someday be going to the mission field, I kept a list of each church where we ministered. As we later began our deputation ministry, I would then contact the pastor of each of these churches to schedule a meeting. Praise the Lord for these contacts that God gave us in many wonderful churches from New York to Illinois, many of whom have faithfully supported our ministry since 1972!

In one of these meetings, at Forrestville, New York, a mother and her teenage son came up to meet me after the service and to share with me his desire to serve the Lord someday. Dr. Michael Grisanti is now a professor of Old Testament at the Master's Seminary in California. Praise God!

CHAPTER TEN

My Life's Partner – Dreams, Hopes, and Reality
1967-1971

While growing up, we had occasionally gone to western New York to visit at "The Farm," the homestead of the Wightmans on my mom's side of the family. We would attend church at the First Day Baptist Church in Richburg, New York. One of the church's charter members was my great-great grandfather Simon Wightman in the early 1800's. My mom had also been saved and grown up in that church. On occasion, we would also attend the West Clarksville Baptist Church in West Clarksville, New York. One of my most vivid memories of our visits in that little church was the time that I noticed a family of six—a mom and dad along with four cute daughters with long blond hair. About ten years later, one of these would become my wife!

The summer after my freshman year at BBS, I attended the Odesega Bible Conference in Machias, New York, because the speaker was Dr. Wendell Kempton, who at that time was the head of the athletic department and basketball coach at Baptist Bible Seminary where I was attending. A certain young lady caught my eye, but she was with someone else and so was I. You guessed it. She was one of those Richmond girls.

At the end of my sophomore year, The Anchormen traveled for BBC for their first summer. We loaded up the old-school Chevy station wagon with our luggage for ten weeks as well as our instruments. It didn't all fit comfortably in the car, so we secured several of the suitcases on the top carrier. We had just started cruising south on Interstate 81 heading to our first engagement of the summer when we heard a strange noise on the roof and an air horn blowing behind us. Our suitcases had become dislodged from the top carrier and were tumbling down the highway behind us. The semi's driver who was following us was slaloming between the careening suitcases! He missed them all and they all stayed latched and in one piece. I actually came to Italy with one of those suitcases, the corners all scrubbed and it wasn't even an American Tourister. We couldn't afford them!

It was a wonderful ten weeks of blessing as we ministered in churches and camps from New Jersey to Michigan and Indiana, but as we finished our tour, I received a call from Dr. Kempton telling me that the first tenor from the other musical group that was touring for BBC that summer—The Defenders—had suffered an appendectomy and that they still had nearly three weeks of ministry left. Would I be willing to continue on tour for another three weeks to help meet this need?

I didn't have to return to a job; there was nothing waiting for me along that line in rural upstate New York. I didn't have a girlfriend. My parents thought it would be a good opportunity to get more experience in serving the Lord in this way, and the school would also reimburse me well for my time, so I decided to stay on the road. I had mixed feelings as I was dropped off with the new group and watched the rest of the Anchormen head on home to their families and sweethearts! It was, however, a great honor to sing with my upperclassmen John Murdock, Tim Wilhite, and Chuck Cole, all of whom have now served the Lord for many years. We ministered in a camp in Illinois as well as several churches in the mid-west. The fact that I had no emotional ties was a great advantage as we traveled on that summer.

As classes resumed in the fall, we were on the new campus at Clark Summit. What a treat not to have to walk all those blocks from the dorm to the main buildings! Jackson Hall seemed immense, and all our classes were under one roof. In addition to traveling each weekend for the school with The Anchormen, I was able to get a job washing pots and pans in the kitchen. It was fun to wash the pots and pans and at the same time watch all the new students as they came to the evening meal. Among them was a cute blond who looked familiar. In fact, she was the one that I had met at camp the summer before... Rachel Richmond. In fact, she was one of the four girls in that family of six that I had seen many years earlier at the West Clarksville Baptist Church! Many an evening meal I spent energetically washing the pots and pans in front of the ground-floor window just hoping to get a glimpse of her!

It didn't take me long to get up the nerve to ask her out. Come to find out, she had graduated from the same high school

(Richburg) that my Mom had graduated from! To make a long story short, I fell in love with that girl almost instantly. In fact, on our first date, I told her that I was going to Liberia as a missionary and if she couldn't see that as a career possibility, just to tell me and I wouldn't waste any more of her or my time building a relationship. She accepted to go out with me a second time, and that evening I told her that I thought that she was the woman that the Lord has chosen for me. Bad mistake! That was too fast! It took months before she would go out with me again.

Meanwhile, Rachel came to the awareness that she had never really experienced the new birth, and she was saved by God's grace while a freshman at BBC! At the annual BBC Missions Conference in February of 1969, she yielded her life to God's service. After getting this news, I was sure that now she would understand God's will for her life (with me), but I soon found out that she needed time to grow in her new-found faith and commitment to do the will of God in her life. At the same time, I needed time to grow in my walk with God as I spent time alone with Him early each morning in the prayer closet of my dorm suite.

The following spring banquet gave me the occasion to invite her to go with me and she accepted. We seemed to be on a roll! The tour of the following summer with The Anchormen was a blessing, but the perfumed letters that arrived frequently at the churches for me as we traveled were especially exciting. That following school year, my senior year, we dated as we had time between her studies, work, and cheerleading and my studies, work, obligations as Student Missions Fellowship President, wrestling, intramural football, and Gospel team obligations.

Since I was president of the Student Missions Fellowship that year, it was my responsibility to lead the missions conference.

This gave me a lot of contact with the various missionary speakers, one of whom was Dr. Willliam Fusco who had served the Lord for two terms in Italy.

One day as I was sharing with him my burden to serve the Lord in Liberia, he jokingly said, "That is great that you are going to Africa, but why don't you stop over in Rome for twenty-five years on the way?" We both laughed, but God took it seriously.

The anchor

december 17, 1970　　　　　　　　vol. xii no.

hiteford sings for supper

p:　Larry Whiteford inspires and entertains Seminarions at
ristmas banquet, held Dec. 4. Bottom: Whiteford joins Presi-
nt and Mrs. Pickering at the head table.

*Scranton's Sheraton Motor Inn provided a beautiful setting
r Seminary's annual Christmas banquet attended by 484 Semi-
rions and guests. After a multi-course turkey dinner, the even-
g was climaxed by the second annual coronation of a Christ-
as banquet king and queen. Also highlighting the program was
musical by Larry Whiteford, "The Singing Pastor" of Niles,
ich.*

Queen Rachael Richmond and King Fred Whitman, de
monarchs elected by the student body, reign at the banqu

*Whiteford is becoming known across the nation for
sual ability to communicate the message of Jesus Christ
music as well as the spoken word. Fulkerson Park Baptis
in Niles, which he founded just eight years ago with a h
people, has grown to an attendance of over 800. Before
ing from Bob Jones University, Whiteford was named t
Who among Students in American Universities and Coll
is kept very busy as a pastor, as well as singing for many
congregations and smaller groups.*

alumnus reports disas

Missionary Linda Short, a 1968 BBS grad, reports f
the recent disaster that struck her field of Pakistan.

Linda writes that although the storm killed nearly
just 25 miles (10 minutes by helicopter) away, no one a
guage school was seriously hurt.

One of her native friends found his brother one of
survivors on a nearby island. As he neared the island, t
of dead bodies almost overcame him. Upon landing, he
impossible to walk without kicking aside bodies cov
ground. Disease is now rampant.

(The school paper reported the Christmas banquet)

I was ever more sure that Rachel and I would serve the Lord together in Africa. In May I graduated with a B.R.E. in Missions and, with The Anchormen, left for our final month's tour to Denver, the GARBC Conference, and back in the old Chevy station wagon that the school gave us to drive. During the conference to save money, we, along with Dr. and Mrs. Pickering and their family, stayed at the Singing River Ranch of evangelist Tom Williams and drove nearly an hour and a half each way to and from the conference. We got back east in time for Roger, Paul, and Chris to get married that summer.

Miss Richmond Will Marry Fred Whitman

Mr. and Mrs. Leslie T. Richmond, West Clarksville, have announced the engagement of their daughter, Miss Rachel Ruch Richmond, to Fred Whitman, son of the Rev. Mr. and Mrs. George Whitman, New Berlin.

Miss Richmond, a graduate of Richburg Central School, is a student at Baptist Bible Seminary at Clarks Summit, Pa.

Her fiance is a graduate of Canajoharie Central School. He received his bachelor of Religious Education from Baptist Bible Seminary where he is studying for his bachelor of theology degree. The wedding is planned for June

On the evening of Labor Day, 1970, Rachel and I were engaged. Her parents had driven four hours from West Clarksville to Clarks Summit to see her and she didn't appreciate my anxiousness to see them leave! As we took an evening walk by the lake behind Jackson Hall, her ring was burning a hole in my pocket! As we got to the goalpost on the soccer field, I decided it was time to score, so I took the ring out of my pocket and asked her to marry me. She was still so upset about her folks leaving to head home (thanks to me), that she didn't accept it with all the excitement that I had thought that she should have.

It was a very busy school year, in which we tried to reconcile studies, work, my being Student Council President and wedding plans. It was rough. However we were married on June 19, 1971.

It was a sunny Saturday in Richburg, New York, and we believe that a wonderful testimony was given as to our call to each other and to our service together for the Lord. Rachel's pastor from West Clarksville and my dad, Rev. George P. Whitman, shared in the ceremony. Of course, the other Anchormen were there with their wives. Paul Plew sang, Roger's wife Carol played the organ, and Chris's wife Debby and Paul's wife Pam were there to give a hand in any way they were needed. Tim Wilhite (from my brief Defenders ministry) and his wife Ruth were also there.

On Sunday night, we visited my former missions professor Pastor Orlan Wilhite at First Baptist Church in North Tonawanda just before going on to the Niagara Falls where newlyweds for many years have spent a night.

After a week's honeymoon in Ontario, participating in Hal and Jan Dirksen's wedding in Kalamazoo, Michigan, and a week at the GARBC Annual Conference in Winona Lake, Indiana, we were at Muskegon, Michigan, to go before the Board of Baptist Mid-Missions for our doctrinal examination. In planning that week at the GARBC National Conference in Winona Lake, I had booked a room that we could afford. You can imagine our surprise when we discovered that many of our friends—the entire group from BBC, Gospel team included—was living in the same building! We were able to evade them for the entire week, and only on the last day did they discover that we were their neighbors when we invited them into our room for dessert!

CHAPTER ELEVEN

A Missionary Needs a Mission
1971

Since the evening as a 12 year-old when I had surrendered my life to serve God, there had never been a doubt in my mind that I would be a career missionary in Liberia, West Africa. The only mission that I ever seriously considered was Baptist Mid-Missions, the agency of missionary Roy "Chick" Watkins, now with the Lord, whom God had used to call me to serve Him as a missionary.

Since I was a missions major, already during my freshman year I was involved in the Student Missions Fellowship led by Dr. William Hopewell Jr. What a blessed time of spiritual growth I enjoyed through being involved in student missions prayer meetings as well as working on the preparations for the annual missions conference.

In my sophomore year, I had the blessing of sitting under Dr. Hopewell's ministry. His long experience of missionary service in Chile and in the Philippines through ABWE put a fire in my soul and a determination to serve the Lord faithfully with my life. As part of the Student Missions Fellowship, we participated for months in early morning prayer meetings as we planned for the annual missions conference. That year, we made a field trip to Philadelphia and the old ABWE headquarters on Race Street. It was an honôr to meet Dr.

Commons, Dr. Amstutz, and others in the home office that day. I also had my first meal in a Chinese restaurant!

One episode sticks in my memory. As we planned for the February 1968 conference, we were challenged to pray specifically for a specific number of students to consecrate their lives to missionary service. We also chose one of the most unlikely students on campus as the object of our secret prayer that God would get a hold of his heart and call him to His service. It was incredible as the invitation was given at the end of that last morning's service to see him go forward to commit his life to missionary service! I wish I could say that he made it to the mission field but he didn't. His later backing down on the promise that he had made to the Lord that morning brought much heartbreak to his wife and family in the years to come.

In my junior year, I was asked to become the leader of the African Prayer Band. That was a great experience as I had further contact with the missionaries of Africa and sought to communicate their burden to others as we met faithfully for prayer. My mission professor that year was Rev. Orlan Wilhite who had served the Lord for many years in the Philippines with ABWE His many experiences, as well as his walk with God, were a great encouragement to me. He and his wife took pity on a poor missions major, and I was a frequent guest in their home. Mrs. Wilhite would cut my hair, and I then got to sit at the table and eat a meal with their family.

During my senior year, my missions professor was Dr. Bernard Bancroft, son of Emery Bancroft, one of the founders of BBS and the author of "Bancroft's Theology." Bernard Bancroft, having been a prisoner of war in the Philippines, had returned there to serve as a missionary and remained there serving the Lord for many years beginning in the immediate post-World War II days with ABWE Although we lovingly referred to his classes as "Early Philippines," his many stories communicated to us his love for the Lord and the importance of a dedication without limits to God's call in your life as well as a commitment to ethics in your missionary career. Who will ever forget his characteristic bow ties? There were several of us in his class who graduated with a B.R.E. in Missions that year who have served the Lord faithfully ever since. Names like Terry Tuffs, Teresa Boyes, and Craig and Elaine Kennedy come to my mind.

I also greatly benefitted from courses from former missionary Bob Richards (EBM Mali) and church-planter Frank McQuade (FBHM). Several years earlier, I had had the privilege of ministering with The Anchormen in his church-plant at Franklin Lakes, New Jersey, the home church of fellow Anchorman Roger Killian. All these men transmitted to me a great love for the Lord and a spirit of sacrifice and faithfulness to the end. I thank God for each one.

In spite of all of my contact with missionaries from ABWE, since I was committed to serving the Lord in Liberia, West Africa, in the months prior to our wedding, Rachel and I made application for missionary service to Liberia with Baptist Mid-Missions. We received our preliminary acceptance and were invited to go before the General Council of Baptist Mid-Missions at the triannual conference at Muskegon, Michigan in mid-July, 1971, not even a month after our wedding!

(Our first picture as young missionaries)

CHAPTER TWELVE

The Last-Minute Call to Italy
1971

Our doctrinal examination went well. President Lewis and the men on the General Council were all very cordial. We were especially encouraged by Dr. and Mrs. Joseph Stowell II who had taken us newlyweds under their wings at the GARBC Conference at Winona Lake a week after our wedding! We were accepted as candidates for missionary service in Liberia, subject to the evaluation at the end of the Baptist Mid-Missions Candidate Seminar at Cedarville, Ohio, which was to commence immediately.

We seemed so young. We hadn't even been married a month yet, but we were sure of the step that we were taking... or were we? The first evening, Dr. Gilbert brought the introductory study. One of the first things he said was, "If any of you wives are going to the mission field on the basis of your husband's call to the field, please re-evaluate the step you are taking. If you don't share your husband's call, when things get tough on the field, you'll say that you weren't called there in the first place and you'll run home to your mother!"

That phrase struck us because Rachel, although she felt definitely called into missions, was not more excited over Liberia than any other field. She was definitely following my leadership in this choice but did have some reservations. During those weeks, we were sent out each weekend to provide music for the "veteran" missionaries who would be preaching. The Lord arranged our schedule so that each weekend we went out with veteran Bill Fusco, who had served in Italy for two terms before having to leave the field because of his wife Lorene's health problems. He was broken over the need of Italy, so tragically overlooked by so many Christians for so many years. As Dr. Fusco poured out his burden for Italy in the churches, we were sitting in the front row and absorbed most of it.

We had been looking forward to fitting into a comfortable field of ministry where Baptist Mid-Missions had a historically and numerically great ministry, just one of many family units. However, it just didn't seem right that Italy, so long under the influence of the Roman Church, should be overlooked by missionary-minded people. However, we were committed to going to Liberia…

The doubts in our hearts continued to rise. We were short with each other. We were one step from going into churches to sell ourselves, our call, our burden, and our future ministry in order to raise financial support so that we could minister in a country where we no longer had the peace of God to go!

Only a week remained of the seminar. We had to know the will of God for us, and we had to know it NOW! Our whole future was hinged on this decision. Were we making the right one? We decided that very evening to spend the entire night separately, each one with the Lord. We had to know His will without a doubt! Rachel stayed in our room, and I found a place in the lounge of the dorm on the campus where we had our room.

Early the next morning, I came back to the room so that we could compare notes. I said," Well, Rachel, what do you think?" She replied, "Oh, no you don't. You are the husband. You need to tell me what God has told you!" I replied, "Rachel, I do not understand it, but in my reading and prayer last night the Lord made it very clear to me that he wants us in Italy." With tears of joy in her eyes, she replied, "Oh, Fred, I was sure that we should go there, but I wanted the Lord to tell you!"

The next morning, I made an appointment to speak with the men from the Baptist Mid-Missions home office who were directing the seminar. Later that day, we sat down and I explained what God had been doing in our lives as it related to our future field of service. Instead of hearing questions and doubts that I had expected to hear from them (after all, we had been accepted by the General Council for missionary service in Liberia), they were expressing enthusiasm. It had been many years since there had been a candidate with Baptist Mid-Missions for Italy. In fact, at this point, none of the other approved agencies of the GARBC had expressed any interest in Italy. So our choice of a mission was still on track. We chose Baptist Mid-Missions knowing that it was the only GARBC approved mission in Liberia, and now we would be going to Italy through them, knowing that they were still the only one of the approved mission agencies working in Italy.

As the Candidate Seminar came to an end, we were excited about what the Lord would be pleased to accomplish for His glory in Italy. Two other couples also expressed their desire to serve in Italy, so a team of three couples headed out on deputation at the same time to raise support to go to a land that, by many evangelical missions, had been overlooked.

Still today we praise the Lord for His leading! Since that hot August day in 1971 at Cedarville, Ohio, we've been through a lot but we've never doubted God's call in our lives!

CHAPTER THIRTEEN

Deputation is Not a Dirty Word,
But It Almost Ended our Missionary Career
1971-1972

As soon as we were back home at Clarks Summit, we began contacting churches and planning meetings where we could present the burden for Italy that the Lord had placed on our hearts. I began with my list of churches where The Anchormen had ministered across the north-eastern states. Of course, the fact that my dad was in his fourth pastorate opened up those churches to us as well. Meanwhile, as we lined up services, Rachel was enrolled in her last year toward her B.R.E. in Local Church Ministry while working part-time in a restaurant, and I was working for the maintenance department of BBC. Because of Rachel's classes, we were forced to do most of our traveling on the weekends, but we were able to get in on some missions conferences.

One of the first missions conferences that we participated in was at Emmanuel Baptist in Toledo, Ohio, in October of 1971. Bill Fusco was the main speaker. During the conference, we were invited to meet with the Missions Committee. That meant that if we did well, we would be supported by Emmanuel. The questions that they asked us were difficult; it seemed like an oral exam at BBC! I didn't think that we had done very well. They had expressed great concern that we, as husband and wife, were currently members of two different local churches. Who would have the final authority over us? As we walked out of the meeting to join the evening service, I said to Rachel, "I know that the Lord is going to send in our support, even if we don't get any from here."

As I walked into the auditorium, feeling like a whipped puppy with his tail between his legs, I looked up to the platform where the head pastor was now seated. When he had caught my eye, he gave me a big wink. I knew that it had gone okay. Ever since then, Emmanuel Baptist has been a faithful member of our support team. By the way, I later joined the West Clarksville Baptist Church, Rachel's church, which became our commissioning church for many years.

Those first few months were very intense. We were so anxious to get to the field that we didn't turn down any invitation to speak, regardless of distance or time. As we went into November, for about two weeks, we were booked nearly every night in services from Scranton to Pittsburg to Portville to Olean to Binghamton.

On Wednesday afternoon, November 19th, after classes and work, we grabbed a sandwich and headed up Route 81 to Binghamton for an evening service. After that ministry, we offered a ride back to Clarks Summit to John Jackson and Paul Byrd, who were from that church and had come home for the weekend. As we approached Clarks Summit in the rain and fog, on that long straight descent on Route 81, my eyes grew heavy and my front left tire went off the road. It was impossible for me to bring it back on to the pavement. It was like I was in slow motion as I saw the guardrail approaching our car!

Our 1968 VW bug hit it with great force. In the impact, our two riders (both wrestlers at BBC) came forward on top of Rachel's seat, pushing her forward and pinning her against the dashboard and into the windshield. My leg was momentarily pinned between the fender and the knob to open the trunk. My chest completely bent the steering wheel out of shape. In an instant, I was able to free myself and free Rachel from the vehicle, laying her groaning body on the pavement. The boys, who had been sleeping, were awakened to the various pains that the accident had inflicted on their bodies too. I cried out to God in the midst of that foggy, rainy, and snowy night. It just seemed like a bad dream, but I knew that it was for real. I cried out to God again.

Within minutes, a car approached southbound on Route 81. I flagged down the driver who "happened" to be a part of the Clarks Summit Emergency Squad and told him what had happened, and then he sped on down into Clarks Summit to get the crew. Very soon, the ambulance was there and we were on our way to Community Medical Center in Scranton.

During the primary examination on Rachel, they found massive hemorrhaging, and a young intern, Dr. Gino Mori, was called in to do exploratory surgery. As he opened her up, he discovered that in the impact, her liver had been lacerated. In that instant, the young Dr. Mori invented a way to sew together her lacerated liver and stop the hemorrhaging. She was the first person that had ever arrived at that hospital still alive with that particular injury, and she was not expected to make it through the night.

I will never forget my first view of her. She seemed to be an angel with that long, flowing blond hair and white gown, but her beauty was partially masked by a mass of tubes that ran in and out of her body. If she survived the first twenty-four hours of critical life-support care, they could then attend to her broken jaw, dislocated hip, and fractured ribs. She was in intensive care for a month. For that entire time period, I could see her for ten minutes every four hours.

The accident was reported on the local news at eleven that night, so many of our friends rushed to my side. Former fellow-Anchorman Chris Hindal came up immediately from Mountain Top, where he and Debby were working in a church plant. My mom and dad drove down from New Berlin, NY, as did Mom and Dad Richmond from West Clarksville, NY The weather was bad. It had turned to heavy snow, but the Lord was gracious to all the travelers. There was an immediate outpouring of love and concern from the faculty and student body at BBC. We didn't know if we would ever go to Italy or not, but we knew that God was faithful. Rachel's anguish in those first hours and days came from the thought that I might have to go to Italy by myself! Praise the Lord that didn't happen!

Many local pastors and pastors of churches that we had visited drove many miles to come and be an encouragement to us, but I found my greatest comfort in the Psalms which I devoured hours on end as I waited in the ICU waiting room for those precious ten minutes that I could be with my beloved. The only unappreciated visit was the well-meaning pastor who came and, after getting permission to have prayer with her, asked her if there was perhaps unconfessed sin in her life that had been the cause of the accident!

Our world had temporarily stopped. Meetings were canceled, and we dedicated ourselves to waiting upon the Lord for the next step. During this time, Student Body President Don McCall led the student body in intense prayer for Rachel's recovery as well as in taking up a large collection from the students and faculty to help with our expenses. When Rachel was moved out of intensive care, I resumed my meetings, and after another two weeks, she was able to leave the hospital. The First Aid Squad of BBC kindly arranged her transport by ambulance from Scranton to West Clarksville near Olean, New York, so that her mom could care for her.

By February, Rachel, still on crutches, was able to return to the deputation trail with me, and by that fall, after just a year of deputation, the Lord had sent in all of our required support. That fact was as miraculous as her survival and recovery, so we definitely saw the hand of the Lord in using that tragedy to get our names before thousands of brothers and sisters in Christ across the country and, through this, touching their hearts concerning the urgency of getting the Gospel to Italy.

Looking back, there are a couple of very interesting aspects of this "accident." Within a two week period, all three of the couples who were on deputation to go to Italy with Baptist Mid-Missions had automobile accidents.

Dr.Gino Mori, who had been guided by God to invent a method of sewing together a lacerated liver in order to stop the hemorrhaging and save Rachel's life, was subsequently invited to speak at many medical conferences in order to explain his procedure. It was so unheard-of for a patient with that particular injury to arrive to the operating table still alive. Rachel, in fact, had been the first of such to do so at the Community Medical Center of Scranton.

Dr. Mori's father had emigrated from the city of Gubbio (near our future home in Perugia, Italy) to Scranton back in the '30s to escape from fascism in Italy. He had supported his wife and two boys the best he could working in the coal mines and shipping grapes from California to make wine for his fellow Italians. Through great sacrifice, he had put two sons through medical school, and they had both become great surgeons, one of which was destined to save the life of Rachel, a future missionary to his people in Italy! It has been our joy to cultivate a friendship with Dr. Mori over all these years.

ORDINATION '72

(Our last Christmas together with family - December 1972)

CHAPTER FOURTEEN

We're Off... to Prison – Homesickness and Culture Shock
1973

January 1, 1973. The time had come! With the missionary conferences, Ordination Council and commissioning by our local church, and the West Clarksville Baptist Church behind us, it was time to leave. It was my little brother Dwight's ninth birthday. We had arrived at the Syracuse Airport accompanied by our families and a group from the Dresserville Baptist Church led by Pastor Craig Golden. We had said our goodbyes through many tears and like two pack horses had carried our carry-ons (briefcase, beauty case, camera bag, tripod, hanging bag, etc...) across the tarmac to the commuter plane that would be taking us to JFK International Airport in New York, where we would be meeting our future co-workers and catching our flight together to Rome.

As we looked out our window toward the terminal, we could see my mom, crying, holding my nine-year old brother, also crying, and we were crying. All the glory of the missionary conferences and the glowing report of what we hoped to accomplish for God's glory in Italy was gone. I felt like I was going to prison for a four-year sentence. I couldn't imagine being away from my family for so long!

Soon we were airborne, and then after touch-down at JFK, we had the challenge of moving all of the things that we had carried on the plane from Terminal Five to Terminal One—

without getting a bus! We had plenty of time and soon met our co-workers who had flown in from Richmond (Ross and Sara Stump, Cherrie, and Chris) and from Winston Salem (Paul and Judy Renigar, Deborah, and Gordon). What a pleasant surprise to also find our dear friends Chris and Debby Hindal with their tiny baby Jody at the gate waiting for us. They had driven down from Mountain Top just to say goodbye. We were moved. As you can imagine, they are among our dearest friends to this day.

Our first trans-Atlantic flight was uneventful and we were soon in a new world.

Praise the Lord that former missionary to Italy Bill Fusco was there at Rome to meet us, help us load our luggage (it all arrived!) in two taxis, and check us in overnight at the YMCA in downtown Rome. We didn't speak a word of Italian and had no idea what we were going to do, but we were very comforted that Bill was there to help us through the loops.

After a dinner of vegetable soup and terrible-tasting "fizzy water," we went to bed. The next morning, we awakened to the sound of car horns and traffic. After breakfast, we rented three vehicles to take us with our luggage to Perugia (Pe-roo-jah). I learned how to drive in Italy that day. Bill Fusco, a veteran of two terms in Italy, drove the first vehicle. My new co-worker Ross, who spoke no Italian, drove the second vehicle, and I, who knew even less Italian, drove the third vehicle. Our job was to keep the three vehicles together as we crossed a very chaotic downtown Rome to get to the motor road on the north side of the city.

Since I spoke no Italian, I was certain that if we got separated in the downtown district, I would have wandered the streets of Rome for years to come. Needless to say, we did not get separated. There were a couple of close calls as streetcars crowded our lane (or vice-versa), but we made it to Perugia, praise the Lord. I was determined that none of those Italians was going to cut me off at the intersection, and that was a valuable lesson with which to begin my driving career in Italy. It is true; when push comes to shove, no one wants to deliberately mark their vehicle!

After checking into the Hotel Astor, an old hotel across the street from the train station in Perugia, we went to supper. Once again, only a plate of pasta for 350 lira because that 1,200 lire seemed too much for a plate of meat and vegetables (about $2.50 according to the exchange back then)!

On January 3, 1973, we woke up to a foggy, rainy, and cold Perugia. It was so depressing that we didn't even want to go out and walk around in our new home. We spent most of our time in our cold, cramped hotel room when we were not involved in registering for classes at the University for Foreigners or looking for more permanent housing.

Our first Sunday in Italy, we attended a small evangelical church in the medieval center of the city and were graciously invited for lunch at the head elder's home, where, with great effort, we came to understand that we had eaten horse. Sorry, Fury, it wasn't that bad!

After two weeks in the hotel, we found housing in the apartment of missionaries George and Annette Murray who, after two years of language study, were returning to the States for six months to visit their supporting churches. That would give us just enough time to get into language study and look for an apartment on our own.

When we were all in our own places, it was time to accompany the Fuscos down to Rome for their return flight to the States. We felt like orphans when they boarded their plane, but the Lord never abandoned us. Praise Him!

(Our apartment on Via Mascagni)

CHAPTER FIFTEEN

Language School – That Big Green Monster
1973-1974

With Bill Fusco's help, we had been able to register for our language classes, and as we started our first day, we were scared but confident that the Lord would help us conquer this giant that loomed between us and the ministry that He had called us to accomplish for His glory. Our school building was a seventeenth-century palace where one of the leading families of Perugia had lived at one time. The main entryway was complete with the stone columns where, centuries before, the horses and buggies had been tethered up. Many of the classrooms had at one time been bedrooms, complete with ancient mirrors and blown-glass chandeliers from Venice. The students' snack bar was in the basement where the stables had once been located.

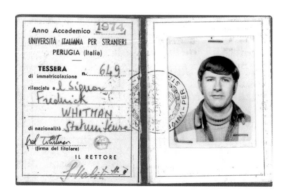

Our first day of language study started on a humorous note. We were late getting to the university and ran up the stairs and into the classroom where we had understood our lessons to begin. When we sat down, caught our breath, and looked around, we discovered that the entire classroom was full of Japanese students! At the break time, we found the right classroom!

When we finally got in our classroom, the fun began. Our professor spoke no English, and anything that we were to learn, we would learn it directly in Italian. In the long run, this was great because it freed us from having to translate mentally from Italian into English and then back into Italian before responding in a conversation. The fun part was dictation. Our professor would speak very slowly so that we could write down every word, but we could not understand why we were always falling behind the others. Every line, we were falling more and more behind! Finally, our Yugoslavian friends explained to us that we were not to write down "lasciare una riga". That simply meant that we were to leave a blank line. When we got that down, we did much better at keeping up!

One of the highpoints of our time of language study was being used of God to bring a Jewish classmate, Cara, to the faith in the Lord Jesus as her Messiah, Lord, and Savior. After only a year and a half of studies, Rachel, now expecting our firstborn, was able to get her diploma from language school. I, after a full two years, was able to finish my final exams just in time to leave for the States for a short furlough.

(Christmas concert at the University for Foreigners - 1974)

Our diplomas, which allow us to teach Italian anywhere outside of Italy, are about the size of a large place mat. We have always been thankful for the men in our home office who encouraged us to spend up to two years but *get the language!* Certainly many of the doors that the Lord has opened to us would not have come to reality had we rushed through the program to "get into the ministry" as many have done in the past.

During the summer of our second year of language school, we were asked to help in a children's camp in northern Italy. That was a great way to practice our Italian. It also brought us into contact with the reality of the lack of discipline as it relates to educating the majority of Italian children! The fact that we insisted that the children clean up their plates of all the food that they had asked for did not make us the most popular among the counselors.

CHAPTER SIXTEEN

A New Missionary in the Whitman Home
1974-1975

Things were pretty exciting in the Whitman home when Rachel shared with me that she was carrying our first child! It came, however, at an interesting time. After our return from the Christian camp in mid-August, 1974, I developed severe pain in my abdomen. A doctor was called to the house who, after his examination, declared that I had a severe case of bronchitis and gave me some pain pills to eliminate the pain I was experiencing, "probably due to eating too many peas". Rachel and our colleagues were not convinced that Dr. Gentile ("Kind") really knew what he was talking about, so they arranged to take me to the Salvatore Mundi International Hospital in Rome on Thursday afternoon, inventing some excuse because I did not want to go. After the preliminary examination, the doctor told me that I had appendicitis but it could be treated with antibiotics. I told him that I had come all the way to Rome—over a three hour trip at that time—so I would rather take it out. "That would be fine," he replied. "However, unfortunately, the surgeon is on vacation and will not be returning until Monday morning when we will schedule the surgery."

On Monday morning as they were prepping me for surgery, I felt something pop inside me. It was very similar to the feeling when we as kids would pop small balloons in our mouths. In surgery, they discovered peritonitis, and, as the surgeon said, he "pulled me up by my hair". During those days of recovery, Rachel was not feeling well either, so we had her do some tests. The doctor discovered that she was anemic and gave her boxes of high-powered vitamins. She took them for about a week and then discovered that she was expecting our first child. You can imagine our anxiety as we lived those nine months knowing about all that high-powered medicine that she had taken in the early weeks of her pregnancy! As for my recovery from peritonitis, after a very difficult two-week convalescence in Rome, we were able to return to Perugia, and I resumed language classes in October.

After finishing work for my diploma in December, we went to the States for a six-month furlough. It was wonderful to visit our families and many of our supporting churches. Knowing the baby's due date, I arranged two weeks before and after the birth so that I could be there with Rachel and the new baby. The due date came and went, and still no baby! I had to resume my traveling schedule. One early Monday morning in late May, after an intense Sunday of ministry at Faith Baptist in Sellersville, Pennsylvania, I was eating breakfast with Pastor and Mrs. David Auckland when the phone rang. It was Rachel.

"Hi, Fred, don't hurry home," (I was about seven hours by car from her), "but my labor has begun!" Believe me, I made that trip from Sellersville, PA, to West Clarksville, NY, in record time so that I could take Rachel to the hospital. In the labor room, however, Jonathan was not in any rush, and after nearly 34 hours of hard labor, he was born on Tuesday morning. As

Jonathan was being born the doctor discovered that his umbilical cord had been wrapped around his neck several times keeping him from coming down the birth canal!

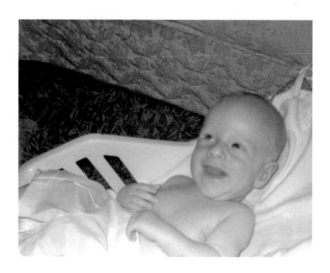

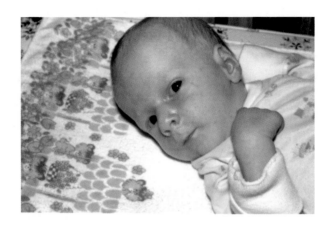

How unfair! As I had planned my furlough itinerary, I had left two weeks at home before and after the baby's due date, but since Jonathan arrived nearly *four weeks late*, the next day after he arrived, I had to leave again for meetings. My "pity party" on the eight hour trip for the Wednesday evening service at the Bible Baptist Church in Shiremanstown, Pennsylvania, was interrupted about an hour north of Harrisburg, when the engine went out on the old Rambler station wagon that I had borrowed from my grandfather for use during furlough. I arrived at the very end of the service, being able to give only a fraction of my presentation, and then had to wait there for a couple of days while my vehicle was repaired. Praise the Lord that He allowed me to get back to Cuba, NY, just in time to pick up Rachel and our firstborn and take them home! We thank the Lord for each of the learning experiences that He has used in our lives to equip us for service.

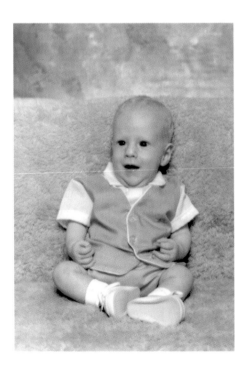

In September of 1975, we came back to Italy with Jonathan David. After arriving in Rome, we learned that there had been a misunderstanding with our co-workers as to the day of arrival, and no one was there to meet us. We took the train to Perugia with our new baby and all the luggage, but the Lord helped us. When we arrived at the Perugia train station, Lucia, our Italian neighbor lady, literally ran a mile from her home to the train station to come and meet us and see the new baby.

CHAPTER SEVENTEEN

We're in Business; But Nobody Knows It!
1976

Upon returning to Perugia with formal language study finished, we were ready (or were we?) to begin our church-planting ministry in Italy. We had been considering the city of Lucca, northwest of Florence, because we had been told that it was a needy area. At the same time, we had been invited by a wonderful church in Rome to go down and do an apprenticeship with them for a couple of years. That would have been a great experience to learn from veteran missionary Bill Standridge, but our mission felt that it would have been more advantageous for the work if we would launch out immediately on our own pioneer outreach. Along with Dr. C. Raymond Buck, our field secretary, and our fellow missionaries, it was decided that we would remain in Perugia. There was no Baptist church in the city and only a very tiny Brethren Assembly for a city of 120,000. It was also felt that as new missionaries with Baptist Mid-Missions would arrive, it would be helpful for them to have a Baptist church with which to fellowship while doing their language study.

We began a Bible study with Villelma, a lady who lived in our town, who had been saved through the Brethren church, as well as with a young couple who had virtually dropped out of that church. We were asked by the elders themselves to try and recover for the Lord this couple as well as be an encouragement to the lady who lived in a very hostile family situation and was not able to regularly go up into the city to attend their services. Villelma has been our most faithful church member all these years!

After several months of Bible studies in the homes, we were finding great difficulty in inviting Italians into that setting. At the same time, a small storefront of about 900 square feet in the same building where one of our families lived became available. The rental was doable, and we decided to take a step of faith even though it was much more space than what we needed. We began working to make some divisions and prepare it for use as a church.

In those months, we met a couple of young American medical students in a very interesting way. One of our Italian neighbors stopped me on the street to tell me that we had some fellow citizens renting an apartment from them. That day, as I was driving down the street, I saw two young men walking together who seemed very American. I stopped the car, introduced myself, and invited them to the house for homemade ice cream. When they found out who I was, they were not too interested, but at my insistence, they were soon guests for a meal in our home.

As Italian Catholic boys growing up in New Jersey, Peter and Larry had been taught not even to walk in front of the Baptist Church, and they would cross the street to avoid it. Now they had accepted an invitation to dinner in the home of a Baptist minister! That first evening in our home, they were like cats on a griddle, and the only mention of God was as we returned thanks for the lovely meal that Rachel had prepared for us. We learned about each other's families in the States and their ambitions to study medicine in a foreign culture since, because of the closed numbers, they had not been able to get into medical school in the States. After a lovely evening together, as was our custom, we asked them to sign our guest book. They signed without giving their addresses in fear that we would come and hound them about "our religion".

In the following week, we invited them over again. They were only too glad to accept as Rachel's home cooking was a nice change from their own. Our approach was still the same. We were determined not to scare them off with too aggressive an approach about the Gospel. We prayed.

On their third visit, shortly after arriving in our home, Larry spoke up. "Aren't you going to tell us about your religion?" With that invitation, we began sharing with them what the Lord Jesus had accomplished on Calvary and why we had dedicated our lives to tell the good news in Italy, a very religious but lost society. Within a few months, both had made professions of faith in the Lord Jesus Christ.

During those months, even though they were very much loyal to the religion of their families, the two of them would come and listen to the preaching in our church services. They felt sorry for us because, for fear of the priest, hardly anyone was willing to come out to our services. Our Sunday morning

101

attendance was between five and ten people. Much has happened in our lives over these many years, but we praise the Lord for the input that He allowed us to have in the lives of these two young men far from home. The Lord gave Larry a wonderful help-meet and three lovely children. He was a deacon in a Baptist church in New Jersey and served the Lord as a Christian physician in Pennsylvania. He has gone on with the Lord.

(Jonathan's second birthday)

CHAPTER EIGHTEEN

This Will Never Happen Again! –
An Airport Miracle
1977

In 1977, it was time for us to take our first regular furlough. The Renigars were still in the Perugia area, so they were able to cover for us at the church. What an undertaking to plan services in thirty supporting churches which covered a geographic area from New York to Illinois and down to Virginia! We also planned to spend the spring semester at BBC so that Rachel could finish her degree program interrupted by our automobile accident in 1971.

We found an inexpensive charter flight that would be flying out of the Rome Ciampino Airport. We stayed overnight at the Stumps', our co-workers at that time in Rome. They would accompany us to the airport in the morning for our flight. We arrived at the airport in good time only to learn that due to some unexpected repairs on the plane, we could not check in yet, and the flight would be delayed for several hours. They didn't know for how long. Our host graciously insisted that he take us back to his house on the other side of the city where we could relax and possibly do some last-minute shopping.

After a couple of hours, as we were sipping tea, I asked if we shouldn't make our way back to the airport. We loaded up the car again and headed around the Ring Road (Raccordo) toward the airport. We hit traffic. The four-lane highway seemed to be a parking lot. After what seemed an eternity, we were finally driving through the gate into the airport. We drove right up to the terminal and hurriedly unloaded the baggage, six suitcases plus our hand luggage. Among the carry-ons was a soft bag in which we had packed a lovely vase which we had bought for my parents' thirtieth wedding anniversary which we had missed during this term in Italy.

When we went into the terminal, there was no longer any information about the flight on the board or at the check-in booth. I ran down to the passport check and asked the policeman where our flight was. He replied that it was on the runway! I replied, "That is our flight!" Since it was a charter flight, if we missed it there was no rescheduling without paying for three new tickets!

He picked up the phone and called the control tower who contacted the plane. They waited on the runway while the three of us were thrown into the motorized luggage cart with our suitcases and carry-ons and were transported out to the plane. The luggage compartment was opened, our luggage was tossed in and the stairs were opened so that we could climb on board. Three seats were found, although not together, and our seatbelts were hooked. Ten minutes after we had driven through the main gate of the airport, we were airborne over Rome! God is my witness. It happened just like that. In our terrorist-ruined world, it could never happen today, but it did that day. As I closed my eyes to thank the Lord for the miracle that he had done for us, I thought about our suitcases and then realized that the soft-shell carry-on with the vase had been thrown in with all the other luggage! Oh well, there was nothing that could be done about it now.

After an uneventful flight (as uneventful as a flight could be with a small child), we arrived at JFK. When we arrived at the luggage claim, our luggage was the first to come out of course —it had been on the top of the pile! The soft carry-on bag was the first, and with fear we opened it; the vase was in perfect shape! Praise the Lord for how He takes care of us, even the little things of our lives! The beautiful hand-painted vase looks so sweet on my mom's piano!

CHAPTER NINETEEN

Two Is Company
1977-1978

During those first six months of travels, Rachel informed me that we were expecting our second child. Since our home base during the first part of furlough was Rachel's family home in West Clarksville, NY, she was able to enjoy her parents' and sisters' company for those months. In January, we moved to Clarks Summit and rented a furnished apartment at what was once called "Hamilton Terraces", next to Rt. 81 north of Clarks Summit. Actually, it was just north of where we had experienced our automobile accident back in 1971.

During the week, Rachel took the classes that she was lacking for her B.R.E. in Local Church while I took classes at the seminary. We took turns babysitting Jonathan. I would rush home from classes so that she could rush back to campus and climb the stairs to her class on the fourth floor of Jackson Hall. Each weekend, we traveled and reported on our first term of missionary service in Italy to our supporters.

Since Rachel's due date was around graduation time, the last few weeks of classes with her various projects were like the old game show "Beat the Clock". On Saturday, she finished her last project for graduation, and late that evening, her waters broke. That was also the weekend before my final exams for the semester of seminary. Starting early Sunday morning, I coached her through hard labor while studying for my Greek

109

exam which was to be on Monday morning. Jeremy was born in the afternoon just in time for me to call and share the good news with someone from Summit Baptist before church started that evening.

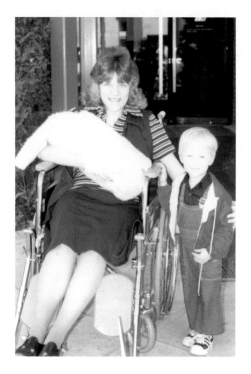

Rachel got out of the hospital on Wednesday and was able to walk to receive her diploma and shake President Pickering's hand on Friday. Since she was in no shape to go up the stairs to the stage, she was given a chair with the professors on stage.

In late August, we returned to Italy with two little missionaries, Jonathan and Jeremy, as well as with two new co-workers with

Baptist Mid-Missions, Allen and Kathy Pick. For the years that they were on the field, they were our closest of friends.

(Visiting brother Duane's family in Germany - 1978)

CHAPTER TWENTY

The Miraculous Invasion of Enemy Territory Through Every Family's Idol
1978-1979

It was wonderful to get back to our ministry and our little flock in Italy, but with two small children, things were very hectic, to say the least. Trying to balance ministry needs with family needs was not easy, and often, I am sorry to say, with the pressure to "succeed in the ministry", the family was neglected.

In December of 1978, something happened which changed the course of our ministry. We received a phone call from the Director of Music at the University for Foreigners where we had attended during our first two years on the field. While we were students, we had participated a couple of times in the annual Christmas program, singing and playing our instruments. Maestro Sabatini explained to us that there were not enough student volunteers to put on a program for Christmas, and he asked if Rachel and I would be willing to come, sing in the choir, and do some music of our own. We were all too glad to lend a hand. The evening of the concert, a camera crew from the largest local TV station, Tele AIA, was there to film the concert.

The next day as I drove by the TV studio in Perugia, I decided to stop and see when the station would be airing the concert. While speaking with the secretary, I felt led, almost tongue in cheek, to offer to be of assistance if they ever needed any religious programming. Before I had even arrived home, they had already called asking when they could interview me on their station.

For months, they had been asking the bishop of the local diocese to send a priest to do something religious on their station, but the church had snubbed them. The religious authorities had said, "We have the people in church on Sunday, why should we bother them in their homes?" The owner, in addition to being offended that they didn't think that his station was important, was also curious to know about the Baptist church since Jimmy Carter, the "Baptist," was president of the United States in that time.

I was interviewed for several weeks on the director's program of local news events. On each occasion, I had the opportunity to speak of our ministry in Italy and the Gospel of Christ that we preached. During that time, many people, some total strangers, stopped me on the street to tell me how much they appreciated what I had to say. Even though I had no training in broadcasting except for singing on my dad's radio program starting when I was five years of age, I saw this as an opportunity to enter thousands of otherwise closed Italian homes. I called the studio and asked for an appointment to speak with the owner.

As I spoke with him, his face lit up when I stated that our church would like to buy some publicity on his station. I was thinking in terms of a thirty-second spot announcement that would run as often as we could afford to pay for it. His response to my request was shocking. He said, "I have ten minutes every day at the end of local news that I need to fill. Would you be interested?"

My first response was, "What would it cost?"

He replied, "How much could you pay?"

As I thought about our financial situation, I had about $150 a month in my work fund that was available, so I replied, "One-hundred and fifty dollars a month." I was asking him to tape and air twenty-four ten-minute telecasts a month for $150! He smiled again and said, "That isn't very much, but I would like to do an experiment. I'll give you a three-month contract for that price." I would have a ten-minute telecast six days a week for the entire three months! I couldn't believe it, especially since Perugia had been under the Papal States for three hundred years prior to being liberated by Garibaldi. Consequently, the Roman Catholic Church was very powerful. I pinched myself to see if I was dreaming. I wasn't, and now I had to decide what I would do on television Monday through Saturday for the next three months. When I saw my co-worker, I said, "What will I do?" He responded, "You have a Bible don't you?" Of course! I named my program "La Bibbia Oggi" (The Bible Today).

I firmly believed that after three months I would be off the air. There was no way that the Roman Church would let me stay on. Since it would be the only opportunity that most of the listeners would ever have to hear the Gospel on television, I decided to make every program count. I made a list of twelve areas of conflict between Roman Catholic doctrine and the Bible, and then each program for twelve weeks, I spoke about them in love.

At the close of each program, I gave our phone number and offered a free Bible to anyone who would call in and request it. For weeks, it was total silence. It was like no one was listening. Finally, the TV station got a phone call. It was from the bishop of the local diocese of the Roman Catholic Church. "Do you remember that TV time you offered us? We decided that we want it." The station owner replied, "I am sorry. That time has been taken by Rev. Whitman. He has a contract and is doing a good job. If you want, I'll sell you another time slot". He ended up giving them a half an hour free of charge each Saturday evening. When I complained to him about paying when they were getting their time for free he replied, "Rev. Whitman, the Catholic Church has many ways of paying." I understood that I should just thank the Lord that I had my time slot, even if we were paying for it. The fact that we had a contract was the only thing that had saved our spot on his schedule of programming.

I couldn't wait to hear the monsignor's program, but I couldn't believe my ears when he took five minutes of his first program to explain who I was and why the Catholic listeners (95% of the population) should not waste their time listening to me! At first, I was upset, but the more I thought about it, the more I realized that if the Roman Church was forced to say something about my program, it was because we were having a great response from the listening audience, even though they did not have the courage to get directly in contact with us. After that little bit of negative publicity from the number two man in the diocese of Perugia, the responses started trickling in! Praise the Lord! Since February of 1979, there have been an average of two telecasts a day up to the present time. That figures out to nearly 10,000 telecasts!

In June of 1979, we had an evangelistic outreach in the center of Perugia with a converted Roman Catholic priest. Franco

Maggiotto had come to faith while an arch-priest (eight priests under him) in the parish of the main cathedral of Imperia, in northern Italy. We had conferences each evening in the city hall in front of the beautiful thirteenth-century fountain in the main city square. We also had the opportunity to participate in a live round-table discussion organized by the television where I had begun my TV program several months earlier. Among the participants, including Franco Maggiotto, was an agnostic university professor, a leader in the local Communist Party, and one of the leaders in the liberal Waldensian church in our city as well as the talk show hosts. It would be a wonderful opportunity to share our faith and have some immediate reaction from the viewing audience, as they could call in with questions for the panel.

As the telecast began, the phone rang, and there was no one on the other end. In those years, if someone called you and didn't hang up, your phone would be blocked until the phone company could intervene. The phone of the studio was blocked, and we didn't receive one phone call in the entire ninety-minute telecast. As helpless as we felt in not being able to get immediate feedback from the viewers, we knew that God was in control. Franco was such a dynamic speaker, and his story of faith and how he left the Roman Catholic Church was so captivating that he basically monopolized the entire telecast. It was incredible. As the program came to an end, each of the members of the panel was asked to give a short summary of the evening. The agnostic university professor, with tears streaming down his face, said, "If there is a God, we've seen Him here tonight."

The next morning, I received a phone call from the director of the station asking me if I had gotten a paper that morning. I hadn't. He just said, "Go out and buy one immediately." When I read the paper, I couldn't believe my eyes. On the front page of the local news, there was a five-column article denouncing the "antidemocratic" television station for having invited a former priest to come and speak against the church when there was no official representative of the Roman Church invited to participate. Actually, the bishop's office had been contacted, but they didn't want to send anyone to be on the program.

Actually, the telecast caused such a stir in Perugia that it was re-broadcast several times in the next week. The following week, however, the Roman Church was given the entire program so that they could smooth out all the waves that were caused by the program. Praise the Lord! The next morning, Pastor Maggiotto left by car to return to his family in northern Italy. He was quite shaken-up as he called me upon his arrival home to tell me that a car with two men had followed him from my home to his, stopping each time that he did along the route. He was thankful that nothing had happened because previously, shortly after leaving the priesthood, he had been beaten and his nose broken.

One of our earliest television responses was from Emilio, who actually had come to faith before he ever saw our telecast.

Emilio had immigrated to France for work and had been taken up with his successful carpentry business with no time for God. One day, as he had been driving down the highway, he saw a billboard with these words: "Come unto me all ye who labor and are heavy laden and I will give you rest... Jesus Christ."

Shortly thereafter, he was involved in an automobile accident where his wife was killed and he lost a leg which was sewn back on at the French hospital. In that time of anguish, he remembered the words of Jesus that he had read shortly before on the billboard and prayed, "Lord Jesus, I don't know who you are, I never had a need to know, but I am greatly burdened down and without hope. Please come in to my life, forgive and receive me as you promised."

After his recovery, he took his disability pension from the French government and moved back to Foligno, his hometown in central Italy. There, he bought a plot of land and built on it a small home for himself. He had a large family Bible that he would put in a gunny sack with a sandwich and go for long walks up the mountain as therapy for his leg.

One day, he was in the house at 2:00 P.M. and saw my program for the first time. He was overjoyed to listen to the message that up to that time he had thought to believe all alone in this world. When he saw the small pocket Bible that I was offering free of charge at the end of my telecast, he realized that it was just what he needed for his long walks up the mountain, so he called us. When Al Pick and I went to meet him for the first time and take him the Bible, he was seated at his table reading Augustine's Commentary on the Psalms. After a wonderful conversation about his opportunities of witness in his city, he took us in his bedroom to see the kneeling bench that he had made in his closet so that he could pray as the Lord has instructed his disciples.

For many years, we were in contact with Emilio, and then we found out that he had gone to be with the Lord several years after the fact. One December, I was delivering our Scripture calendars to a family who had asked for ten of them. As I questioned the lady of the house as to how she had heard of us and why she wanted so many, she told us that she was Emilio's granddaughter and had learned from him to appreciate the Scriptures. She went on to tell us about his death.

In his old age, he had started to slow down and was soon bedridden. For months, he had not gotten out of bed but suddenly one day, he called his daughter-in-law who was taking care of him and with great insistence asked her to bring him his new suit and his teeth. She said, "Where do you think you are going? You are not going anywhere." He replied, "Oh, yes, I am. I am going to meet my Savior, and I want to be all dressed up for Him." She obediently dressed him up and put his teeth in for him. No sooner had she finished than he went to be with his Savior! Some time earlier he had given me a picture that had been taken of him with his arm around the television during one of my telecasts. I was his pastor.

CHAPTER TWENTY-ONE

Three Is Not a Crowd!
1979-1980

In the fall of 1979, Rachel told me that she was expecting our third child! Our already-busy life with two small children (Jonathan was four and Jeremy was one and a half) as well as with the church work was about to get busier. At that time, I still went to the gym a couple times a week to work out with the local judo team. One evening at a workout, I dislocated a shoulder. That definitely added another dimension to our life as my wife, great with child, now had to bend down and tie my shoes! I decided that it was time that I put that sport behind me as my wife needed all the help that she could get from me and she didn't need me to add to her work load.

During all this time, I carried on the television program and follow-up of those who contacted us as well as the preaching and discipleship in the local church. At that time, we had some co-workers, so some of the work was divided up with the others. I don't know how Rachel made it through this time as I was away a lot with many visits to TV contacts spread over a four-province area of central Italy.

Finances were tight, and in order not to give up the television opportunity, we had decided to come home on an emergency furlough in order to raise funds to keep the telecast on the air. It didn't take Rachel long to pack our suitcases when I told her that we would need to go to the States. That week, however, while I was still finalizing our flight reservations, an anonymous donor sent in the money to keep the program on for a year, as long as we would remain in Italy and not take a furlough at that time. We rejoiced in the Lord's provision, but I can't say that Rachel was overjoyed to unpack the suitcases and call her mom to tell her that we would not be coming home after all.

In 1979, co-workers Paul and Judy Johnson as well as Tom and Linda Jones arrived. Veteran missionaries Carlo and Polly Feriante also returned to the field. This offered new opportunities and challenges as it related to reaching out into areas where we had contacts by means of the television ministry.

On Sunday, May 4, 1980, Joshua was born in the new hospital in Assisi about twenty minutes from our home. It was a very special time for us since Rachel's mom and dad got to be with us and help out during those days. It was a stretching time for us all as Rachel only had two hands to hold three boys in church. Praise the Lord that Jonathan learned early on how to do puzzles, and that kept him occupied and quiet.

CHAPTER TWENTY-TWO

The Second Beachhead by Means of Marconi's Miracle
1980-1981

By 1980, it was evident that we did not have enough support to sustain the expense of the television ministry. Our work fund was depleted, and our personal funds with the mission were going further in the hole each month, so we planned a special furlough to seek new support for this important outreach.

Shortly before leaving for the States, we received a visit from Missionary Arthur Weins, a pioneer missionary who had been in Italy since 1949. He had founded Back to the Bible's Italian branch (Voce della Bibbia) and through that had been instrumental in starting many of the Christian radio stations in Italy. In the days before his visit, I had been approached by a large commercial radio station in Perugia about doing a live program each evening from 10:00 to 11:00 P.M. The price tag was about $5,000 for the year's contract. Although we had no money, I was considering it.

When Arthur heard about that opportunity, he told me that for the same money, we could start our own station and be on the air 24 hours a day! That encouraged me, and Paul Renigar, our co-worker at that time, to consider raising the money for this project. As I planned my short furlough, I was able to get a special round-trip air fare which, for only $100 extra, would get me in and out of ten other cities in the continental U.S.A.

Our transcontinental flight to the States with three small children and all the luggage was an experience. The boys were good, and I am sure that many fellow travelers were amused at watching us. I don't believe we slept too much on that flight. Praise the Lord for Mom and Dad Whitman, then ministering in Latham, New York, who could make the three-and-a-half hour trip to New York City to JFK Airport to pick us all up with their van.

(Our family on furlough visiting Dad and Mom Whitman –
Latham, New York - 1981)

I had contacted friends and relatives in Washington D.C.; Orlando, Florida; Houston, Texas; St. Louis, Missouri; Des Moines, Iowa; and Los Angeles and San Francisco, California to line up ministry opportunities in each of these new areas. It was a long time to be away from Rachel and the three small children, but she was staying with her family in West Clarksville, New York, and I knew that she would be well taken care of by them. New support was added for the media ministry in Florida, Texas, Missouri, and California for which we praised the Lord. More times than not, I forgot to mention the possible radio project since our needs for the television ministry already seemed overwhelming to some, but when we prepared to return to Italy after six months in the States, the Lord had provided about a thousand dollars a month of new support for the television ministry as well as the five-thousand dollars that we needed to begin our own Christian radio station.

Upon returning to Italy, we heard that the Italian government would soon have a law governing private radio broadcasting, and so we worked feverishly to be able to be on the air prior to the December 31, 1980 deadline. We actually began broadcasting on December 27, 1980. Radio Luce (Radio Light) was on the air! Actually, the law regulating private broadcasting didn't pass until 1990!

We went on the air with a 250-watt transmitter and an antenna on top of our two-story building. We had an auto-reverse reel-to-reel and three cassette decks hooked up to a solenoid and a timer. When the cassette decks were stopped by the timer, the solenoid which controlled the reel-to-reel kicked in and the music began. It was very primitive because, when the time dictated, the tapes would stop in the middle of a song without being faded down, but at least the Gospel programs were going on according to a schedule, and the cassette decks would even rewind the program tapes so that they would be ready to go again if no one got to the station in time to change the tapes.

We were covering our town of San Sisto, our side of the city of Perugia that was exposed to the antenna, and Assisi, and that was about it.

In the month of June, our signal was very disturbed by another signal, but our technicians moved our antenna up on a mountain above Perugia and we bought a 1,000-watt transmitter. A few days after the new transmitter was in place (we hadn't even paid any money down on the $20,000 that it cost), we had a tremendous electric storm, and we were off the air. So were the other two stations who shared the tower with us. Within an hour or so, we were back on the air, so I didn't give it much thought. The next week when I went to tape my telecast, though, the technician who taped my program and also was the technician for the television station told me the rest of the story.

When their station went off the air after a large lightning bolt hit the tower, he went up to see what the damages were. Their television transmitter was burned to a crisp. Another large radio station that shared the tower had also lost a very expensive transmitter. He noticed that our fuse box had popped, but when he turned it back on, Radio Luce came back on the air. God had miraculously protected our new transmitter! When he saw that, being familiar with my Bible program since he was the technician that frequently taped it at the studio, he said, "Only to Whitman could something like this happen." Praise God for His watch-care over our transmitter before we had even paid for it!

Very soon after we had upped our power and moved our antennas up on the mountain, we started getting menacing phone calls from another radio station which claimed that we were broadcasting on their frequency. We knew that when we began broadcasting the band was open, and we had checked with the police and no one had registered that frequency. In those days, a new couple began attending our church. Their casual look was very deceiving. They were both lawyers, and he was a law professor at the University of Perugia. As they left church one day, they casually said, "If you ever need any legal counsel, please don't hesitate to ask us."

The very next week, we got notification that we were being taken to court by the radio station that claimed that we had stolen their frequency! This station happened to be the official radio station of the Communist Party which was ruling our province! As soon as we were notified, I called one of the men of our church and he gave me the name of the best (and probably most costly) lawyer in Perugia. I then called the law professor who had visited our services the Sunday before. He referred me to one of his most brilliant former students and the law firm with which he worked. It ended up being the same law firm. The only difference is that because we had been referred to him by his former professor, our fees would be a fraction of what we would normally have paid.

The morning of the first hearing arrived. As I walked into the judge's office, I was full of fear and tried to keep my confidence in the goodness and the sovereignty of God, but being a foreigner and a non-Catholic, I didn't have much going for me. To my surprise, as I entered the judge's office, he looked up from his desk over his half-glasses, and as he saw me, his face brightened and he rose to his feet. "Rev. Whitman, what a privilege to meet you. I have followed your program on television for some time!" That certainly didn't mean that we would win the case, but it did help to settle my nerves! God was in control!

The hearings dragged out for several years, one every two or three months. They brought witnesses; we brought witnesses. At the end of the hearings, some very interesting information came to the forefront. It was true that the Communist station had broadcast on that frequency before we did. However, they had never registered it with the police. At a certain point, they had not paid their electric bill for their transmitter, and the power company had cut off their power. Consequently, for several months, they had not been on the air. In that period of time, we had found the empty, undeclared frequency and had claimed it, declared it at the police station, and begun broadcasting.

The judge's decision read like this: "If you abandoned an expensive pen along the side of the road and didn't go back to claim it while, in time, another person found it, you would have no claim on it being your pen since you had not manifested any desire in keeping it. The said frequency was abandoned by Radio Perugia Uno and then found by Radio Luce; therefore, it belongs to Radio Luce." This decision set precedence in Italian courts and was published in their official national law journal, thus giving Radio Luce not only a right to that frequency, but a right to exist! Praise the Lord!

CHAPTER TWENTY-THREE

It Is a Girl!
1983

Jonathan, Jeremy and Joshua proudly announce the birth of their littlle sister,

Elisabeth Rachel
(Means: consecrated to God)

She was born sunday morning, August 7, 1983 at 4,10 at Perugia, weighing 6 lbs. 11½ oz. She was 19 ½ in. long with hazel eyes and blond hair.

"Take heed that ye dispise' not one of these little ones; for I say unto you, that in heaven the angels do always behold the theface of my father."
Mattew 18.10

Thank you, 'Lord, for this gift of love. Give us wisdom to bring her up according to the principles of Your word. Amen

Gionathan, Geremy e Joshua sono orgogliosi di annunciare la nascita della loro sorellina,

Elisabeth Rachel
(Significa: consacrato a Dio)

É nata domenica mattina, 7 Agosto, 1983 alle ore 4,10 a Perugia. Pesava 3 kg. e160 g. ed era lunga 49 cm. ha gli occhi azzurri e i capelli biondi.

"Guardatevi dal disprezzare alcuno di questi piccoli; perché io vi dico che gli angeli loro, nei cieli vedono del continuo la faccia de' padre mio."
Matteo 18,10

Grazie Signore, per questo dono del tuo amore. Dacci sapienza nell'educarla secondo i principi della Tua parola. Amen

The Whitmans

With three boys—seven, four, and two years of age—the news that Rachel was expecting our fourth child seemed a little overwhelming. We were a long way from our families with no grandparents to lend a hand. There was no time for Rachel to help out in the "ministry" as she had done before we began having a family. The ladies were already complaining that they didn't have a ladies' Bible study any more. We would soon be in need of a furlough, and I couldn't imagine moving the suitcases for the entire crowd, including a new baby, to say nothing of traveling the furlough circuit as a family of six. As much as we were loved by our partners in ministry, few people were up to having six overnight guests in their home!

As the blessed event approached, Mom and Dad Whitman made plans to come over to help out for a few weeks. It was their turn since Mom and Dad Richmond had come over for Joshua's birth. Our concern was that Rachel would go overtime in her pregnancy, as had been the case with the first three boys. The Saturday evening prior to Mom and Dad Whitman's departure from Latham, NY, we had an appointment with the doctor. Rachel's regular obstetrician had broken his finger, and so we had to go to a new doctor in the final days of her pregnancy! The examination went well, but she assured us that it could be a week or two before the baby would come. We were a little concerned that my folks would come and go before the birth of the baby. We had experienced a similar situation before with Joshua being born halfway through the two-week visit of Rachel's parents.

On our way home from the appointment, on a curve just before our street, a speeding car took the corner wide and we narrowly missed having a head-on collision. That shook us up quite a bit, but we made it home, got the kids to bed, and finished preparing for the Sunday ministry. During the night, Rachel woke me up to tell me that her waters had broken. Wow! We left for the hospital complete with newborn baby clothes—for a boy. There was no chance that we would get a little girl. Later that day as I was with Rachel in the delivery room, I got to tell her, "It's a girl!" What a wonderful surprise Elizabeth Rachel was for us. She didn't even complain about coming home dressed as a little boy. I was also able to get the news to my folks before they headed out for their flight to Italy that they had a new granddaughter.

The Whitmans

• PERUGIA

Field Address:
C.P. 34
06080 S. Sisto (PG)
Italy

Baptist Mid-Missions
4205 Chester Avenue
Cleveland, Ohio 44103

Fred and Rachel,
Jonathan, Jeremy, Joshua and Elizabeth

CHAPTER TWENTY-FOUR

Italian Musical Studies for the Children – A Great Investment for the Future
1981-1996

As our children became school aged, we didn't know how they would handle Italian schools. As missionary parents, however, we felt that it was important for our ministry, as well as for the happiness of our children, that they be a part of something in the Italian culture. At their young age, that meant the Italian school system. We praise that Lord that he called us to a culture where the educational system is advanced and among the best in the world. That made this choice a lot easier for us.

In our situation we did not believe that home-schooling was an option. Neither of us felt that we could afford to take time away from our pioneer ministry among the Italians to adequately prepare our children academically for their future. Our children also needed to feel a part of something in their difficult role as M.K.s on a foreign field. As a missionary couple, we had decided to cut the umbilical cord from our home culture to become as Italian as we possibly could, to reach the Italians for Christ. This meant for us letting our kids sink or swim in a very difficult educational system like that of Italy. After nearly forty years in Italy, I have to say that the American missionary families who chose to home-school their children have not lasted, and their children did not return to Italy as missionaries.

Amidst fears caused by some horror stories of American children in Italian schools that we had heard, we knew that we would have to constantly be with our kids and monitor them through the educational process. If they couldn't make it, we were ready to consider alternatives. We prayed that would not be the case, as we had already decided as newlywed missionary candidates that we would not, under any condition, send our kids thousands of miles away to a mission school for their education. God gave that responsibility to us as parents.

We put Jonathan in Italian nursery school for a few months, and then it was off to first grade. It wasn't always easy. One day, he returned home very upset mumbling, "I am going to tear that page from my notebook!" When we finally got him calmed down, he explained to us that his teacher had physically forced him to write in his notebook, "Mary is the Mother of us all."

That next day, I went I to speak with the teacher. She was very apologetic. She had thought that Jonathan was only trying to be a rebellious first-grader. When we explained that we were Evangelical Christians and did not worship the mother of our Savior, she apologized. She stated that in all her thirty years of teaching, she had never had a non-Catholic student in any of her classes. For that reason, she had not known how to react to Jonathan's refusal to write a prayer to Mary in his notebook.

After that time, things went somewhat better, although during the times of "Religious Instruction" (and there is only one religion for most Italian public schools), Jonathan either sat in the corner of the classroom or out in the hall, as if he was being punished for some reason. I know that the Lord used that experience to build his character and that of his siblings into the good soldiers that they have become for the Lord Jesus.

Soon, it was Jeremy's turn to start school. Fearing that he would lose a year of school during the up and coming furlough, we had him study the first grade privately, and he, after taking an exam, went immediately into the second grade.

Joshua was close on the heels of his older brother, so it was natural that he would go into the Italian system, and two years later, coming up on another furlough, it was Elizabeth's chance to start a year early as Jeremy had done. I don't want to give the picture that it was easy. Our children struggled. They didn't have parents who knew Italian well enough to help them with their homework as the Italian parents did for their children. They were always "the Protestant Americans", which was not easy in a total Roman Catholic and strangely leftist society.

There were many struggles and tears from being the "outsiders". There were many opportunities to witness to their faith since their daddy was on television every day talking about a faith that was so far removed from the Italian religion. However, in all of this the Lord gave grace, and they all grew up knowing what it meant to trust the Lord in those difficult times and using their being different to share what the Lord

Jesus could do in and through the lives of those who know Him personally.

As Jonathan neared completion of his elementary school, we began thinking about his middle school. In Perugia at that time, there was an excellent Junior High School that was affiliated with the Francesco Morlacchi Music Conservatory. The catch was that you had to study an instrument to get in. That was fine with us as we wanted our children to study music anyways. Jonathan had already begun studying trumpet, but we decided

143

to switch him to French horn. Although it would be much more difficult, it would give him many more opportunities to play professionally. That ended up being a great choice!

As Jeremy came close to finishing his elementary school, we applied for him to enter as well. He would do trumpet. About two weeks before his entry proficiency exam, Jeremy came down with appendicitis and had to have an appendectomy. That was not something that we would have asked for right before he had to do that exam. If he couldn't do it, he would have to wait another year to begin junior high in the music conservatory! Jeremy's entry exam was only a few days after having been released from the hospital.

Anyone who plays a wind instrument knows how important it is to use the diaphragm. Having had a large incision the week earlier would not make it easy. The Lord helped Jeremy, and he did very well. He played the piece that he had prepared and was able to sight-read as well. One of the professors on the commission asked him what his range was. Jeremy replied, " It used to be much higher." They immediately asked what he meant by "it used to be". When he answered that he had been operated on the week before appendicitis, they couldn't believe it. Needless to say, Jeremy was accepted, and over the years, with a lot of work, became a great trumpeter, much better than his dad.

Joshua also began to study the trumpet, but when it was time for him as well to enter the junior high and the music conservatory, he wisely switched to the trombone. It had been my dream from when the children were small to someday play brass quartets with my boys. I could almost see that dream becoming a reality. Joshua was also accepted at the conservatory and through his studies there became an excellent trombonist.

It was soon Elizabeth's turn to begin Junior High School, and she decided to go with the flute. Actually, a bass tuba would have been better for the Whitman Brass musical group, but the flute was more feasible for a young lady. Elizabeth became a very accomplished flautist and has used her talent much for the Lord in these years.

One interesting experience of many comes to my mind of our years of involvement with the Junior High School of the Morlacchi Music Conservatory. For the last two years that Elizabeth was in the school, I was actually the president of the school board and, in that capacity, represented the school in meetings in Rome with the Italian Minister of Education. I don't know if an American had ever been given that responsibility before that time or not, but I was privileged to be there. In those years I was also able to record and air on Radio Luce numerous concerts by the orchestra of the conservatory.

CHAPTER TWENTY-FIVE

The First Split of a Church That Wasn't
1988

The work went ahead slowly, in spite of the fact that our telecast, "La Bibbia Oggi" (The Bible Today), was being seen a few times each day on several local stations. One of our problems was that in a desire to grow, people had been brought into our fellowship who were not Baptists. Although the preaching of the Word was appreciated, family and emotional ties to the church that had been left behind were still very strong. The situation came to a head thanks to an interdenominational missionary who was fellowshipping in our church. When he decided to go to another church so that he could present his ministry in more churches of Italy and not be limited to the Baptists (few and far between), we relieved him of his duties in leading our youth ministry.

About a month later, without any warning, our entire youth group (with the exception of our son, Jonathan) did not show up for the Saturday night youth meeting. The next morning, following the worship service when I asked the older member of the youth group why no one had come to the youth meeting the night before, he told me that they had decided to go up to the other church for their youth meeting because they liked the way that other missionary did it.

In about four weeks, once again with no warning, we went to the Sunday morning worship service and about twenty-five of our forty regulars were missing. They had decided to follow their teens to the other church. We had not yet organized into a local church, and it was evident that it would be a long time before that would now happen.

(The church family in 1988.
Is Jeremy already looking at Francesca?)

We praise the Lord for His help and encouragement in those days. I was so thankful for having grown up in the parsonage where we as a family had lived through some very difficult times. It was no surprise to me when I saw how wicked and nasty people can be toward God's servants even though they claim to be followers of the Lord Jesus. During that time, my sweet wife organized a 40th birthday party for me, but I have to admit, I wasn't in the mood to celebrate!

The temptation to throw in the towel was great, but the following words of my Lord echoed in my head: "Occupy 'til I come." I am so glad that I obeyed. I would hate the thought of letting someone else be in my place to enjoy the blessings that the Lord had intended for me.

CHAPTER TWENTY-SIX

The Birth Pains of a Local Church
1990-1995

After a long series of expository messages in preaching through the book of Acts, we were approaching furlough, and since the church had grown back up considerably, we decided to move ahead toward the organization of a local Baptist church.

We studied through a Covenant and a Doctrinal Statement. That was a new experience for our folk, none of whom were coming from a Baptist background; most of them had been saved out of Catholicism. Twenty of us signed the doctrinal statement that day.

During our furlough of 1990-1991, Dick, a young man from our Baptist Mid-Missions work in Holland, came down to live in our home and run the radio. At the same time, there was a young couple who was considering Italy as a mission field who came over through Baptist Mid-Missions to work in the church during our absence. They also lived in our home.

While we traveled in the States for ministry, the Lord touched a young lady's heart to come a give a hand with the radio. She got support and came to Italy for a two-year term of service. As her first Christmas in Italy arrived, she asked if she could go back home for the holidays. How could we say no to that? When she came back after the new year, she announced that she had gotten back together with her old boyfriend.

Consequently, she would be leaving at the end of her first year with us.

When the time came for her to leave, I accompanied her to the train station and then came back home. I walked into the station, and while standing in front of the automation system, I began to cry and talk to the Lord. "Lord, you know that I can't do it. Please help me." My sense of helplessness grew to the place that I decided to close the radio station. The laws had been changed concerning the regulation of private broadcasting, and there were so many new documents to present that I just felt it was impossible. I called a special church business meeting, explained my feelings, and asked the church to close the station! Sensing my desperation and seeing no one to help me out in this situation, as any congregation who loved its pastor would have done, they voted to close the radio station as I had asked.

The next morning, I went to talk with our lawyer to explain that we had decided to close the station. This lawyer has been with us from the very beginning—from that first lawsuit that the Radio of the Communist Party had unjustly brought against us. He said, "You can't just close the station! You have already made a request for your frequency, and the government has already begun its census process. You can't shut down the station. You must find a way to finish the application process." So I called another special church business meeting and we rescinded the decision that had been made. I then asked who would help me do the documents. One of our members, Maria, who had a business of her own came to me afterwards and said that she would help me.

Over a period of weeks, we gathered all the documents necessary and were able to officially apply for our broadcasting license. With no outside help for the radio, Rachel was always on call. If there were any problems in the radio, I would call her, and she would need to go into the studio and try and fix it. It got so that if the phone rang, she didn't answer it; she just went in to the radio to see what was wrong!

In those early days, there were no cell phones, so if there was a problem at the station, I had to look for a phone booth, hoping that it would work, and then call home.

The years sped by, and soon it would be time for Jonathan to go to the States for college. After receiving his diploma from the Italian High School in Languages as well as his diploma in French Horn from the Francesco Morlacchi Music Conservatory in Perugia, Jonathan was ready to leave home. In the months before our furlough Jonathan participated in a music contest among professional musicians who had all received their diplomas from music conservatories around Europe. He worked very hard memorizing horn concertos by Beethoven and Strauss.

To our amazement and joy, Jonathan won first place among all wind instruments in our province of Perugia. He then won first place in all of central Italy. He then went on to the European finals in Rome as the only brass player to reach the finals. It was a wonderful experience for him as he made final plans for college in the States. Thanks to Dr. Richard Stewart and contacts with the Grand Rapids Baptist College Music Department, Jonathan was offered a wonderful scholarship to go there and participate in their music program.

Several years earlier in a phone conversation with Dr. Stewart from the music department, he had asked about the possibility of bringing a choir on a tour to Italy. I told him that we would not be interested in hosting a tour for a choir to sing a lot of songs in English, but if they would be committed to singing at least half of their songs in Italian, we would consider it. Doc replied, "That's a piece of cake! My kids sing in Italian all the time."

The first choir tour in Italy was soon in the planning stages. In the early '90s, Perugia had officially become a sister-city with Grand Rapids. This relationship between the two cities gave us some wonderful opportunities over the next fifteen years to do concerts sponsored by the city as well as many meetings with city officials. The main concerts would be videoed and then aired on my telecast as well. On one of those occasions, Tiziano, one of the men in our church, brought an unsaved friend with him. Ivano had been a friend of his during his old life of substance abuse. The concert was his first contact with the Gospel.

A few months later, Ivano was diagnosed with the HIV virus, and his days would be very limited. Tiziano faithfully visited him, and one evening he called me to come and visit with him; Ivano had put his trust in the Savior and wanted to talk with me. I never had seen such a glorious conversion! That rough, foul-mouthed drug addict had come to faith and understood the grace of God in his life. By this time, he was totally bed-ridden, and his days were spent in listening as Tiziano and I read the Scriptures to him. His greatest desire would have been to come to the church and give his testimony of faith before all of his new brothers and sisters and follow the Lord in Believer's Baptism, but for this twentieth-century thief on the cross, like the one in the first century, it was not to be. Ivano died exactly thirty days after he had repented of his life of sin and trusted Christ as his Lord and Savior. I am looking forward to seeing him in Heaven someday.

The Whitmans

Perugia

Field Address:
C.P. 34
06132 S. Sisto (PG)
Italy

Fred and Rachel
Jonathan, Jeremy, Joshua and Elizabeth

Your missionaries to Italy
establishing local Baptist churches

Baptist Mid-Mission
P.O. Box 308011
Cleveland, OH
44130-8011

CHAPTER TWENTY-SEVEN

In the Hour of Need, God's Provision of an Italian Co-worker So That We Could Go to America 1995

As we made plans for furlough and Jonathan's first year in the States for college, there was a big problem. We had no one to manage Radio Luce. Leadership in the local church was also very shaky. In the spring of 1995, I attended an Italian Christian Workers' conference. As we had a time for sharing prayer requests, I spoke of the dilemma that we were facing as far as furlough and our replacements were concerned. After the prayer time, one of the missionary pastors came to speak with me.

There was a young lady in his church who had graduated from the Bible School in Rome and wanted to serve the Lord with her life. She had been saved through a Christian radio ministry in northern Italy and was really burdened to serve the Lord in that way. Maria Luisa came to us the following Easter weekend and met our church folk, and it was love at first sight. She could live in our home, feed Julius Caesar, our cat, and keep an eye on the radio. What an answer to prayer!

Plans proceeded as it related to lining up services in nearly sixty supporting churches from New York to Florida to Texas to California. We had a new missionary couple with Baptist Mid-Missions who could work together with one of our members who was bi-lingual to carry on the services and keep the church running in good order… we thought.

When we arrived in the States to begin furlough, our home church advanced the money to buy a van for our use. That was a great help. I took it to a shop to have cruise control put on as I didn't want the stress of trying to keep my speed down on the highway. The van was ready for us to take it on our first Sunday ministry. At the time, we were with my folks in Latham, and our drive to the morning service was a short one. We loaded the instruments and family into the van and took off down the highway. As we were crossing the bridge into the city, the vehicle lost power, and immediately, smoke began pouring out from around the hood. As quickly as I could, I rolled to the end of the bridge and to the right curb at the intersection. By this time, the van was filing with smoke, and flames were coming out from around the motor. We all jumped out of the car, grabbing our instruments the best we could. A deli was open across the street, and I was able to call the fire company as well as my brother-in-law, Doug, to come and pick us up to take us on to our appointment at the church in Rensselaer, NY.

In the car, we had been listening to the tape of our new slide presentation which we were to have premiered that morning. I remembered the tape only after the firemen had arrived to put out the blaze. When the fire was out, I asked for permission to get back in the van and get my jacket which was hanging behind the seat. I also thought of the tape that I had left in the tape player in the dash. I took the tape out, and it wasn't even hot. We were able to use it that morning in our presentation. Praise the Lord!

The next week, we were supposed to drive on west to Rachel's mom and dad's in West Clarksville, New York, and then on to Grand Rapids to get Jonathan enrolled at Cornerstone College for his first year of school, but it all seemed up in the air at this time. Praise the Lord that the insurance company settled in two days. Meanwhile, my dad had found another lovely van for sale which ended up being nearly the same price as the insurance settlement. By the end of the week, we were in West Clarksville, and in perfect time, we had delivered Jonathan to his appointment at college. Another reason to praise the Lord!

That trip to Grand Rapids was a new experience for us. We had known for many years that someday our children would grow up and leave home to go to college, but that day came all too soon! It was comforting to us to know that God had provided room and board and a music scholarship through the kindness of Dr. and Mrs. Richard Stewart and the music department of the college, but it was still tough to leave him out there all by himself. We would still be in the States on furlough for the entire school year, so it seemed a gradual separation for us.

We were three months into our year's furlough when we received a phone call that informed us that the new missionary couple that we had left to tend the church along with another couple had "left the church." The church seemed at the brink of a total collapse. We didn't know if we should cancel furlough and go back to Italy or not. God intervened once again, and with help from the Bishops—missionaries with Evangelical Baptist Missions in Ancona—our faithful few at Perugia were committed to keeping the church together in our absence. They encouraged us to finish our furlough. They would hold the fort until we returned. Miraculously, the church was still alive—hurting, but alive when we returned from furlough. It took the entire next term to get the church back to where it had been when we left for furlough.

CHAPTER TWENTY-EIGHT

Whitman Brass and Furlough Ministry
1995-1996

Since those early years when the Lord started giving us children, I had had a dream of one day playing music together with my children. We had a wonderful music school that each of them was able to attend. Very early in the musical experience of our children, we involved them in the music of our little church in San Sisto.

With the three boys who studied brass, very soon we were playing quartets. For several years, we did a Christmas concert for the prisoners at the prison in Orvieto where I have had a ministry since 1986.

Whenever we went to the states for furlough, they were always readily welcomed by the music department of the Portville Central School.

In the fall of 1995, we were invited by Pastor Ken Spink to do a concert at the Christmas banquet of the Berea Baptist Church in Berea, Ohio. They have supported the ministry in Italy for many years, and it was a joy to us to be able to minister in that way. We then did Christmas concerts at Haddon Heights Baptist Church as well as first Baptist Church of Willingboro, two other of our supporting churches. Since we had practiced so much, we decided to do something very special. To celebrate our twenty-fifth wedding anniversary, we did a CD of the pieces that we had prepared for the concerts. We thank the Lord that He used our music in this way to be a blessing to many who have supported our ministry for so long.

(The album we recorded for our 25th wedding anniversary)

In February of 1996, I was asked to speak at the missions conference at BBC. We left Jeremy, in his senior year at Portville High School, Joshua, in his sophomore year, and Elizabeth, in the eighth grade, with their grandparents so that Rachel could come with me. On Wednesday night, we were out in area churches for their mid-week services, and a tremendous ice storm set in. As we got back to the campus, the security guard stopped us to tell us to call home; there had been an accident.

When we got a hold of Rachel's mom, we found out that Jeremy and Joshua had been involved in an automobile accident, skidding on ice and rolling the vehicle. Joshua was fine, but Jeremy was in the hospital with head injuries and loss of short-term memory. Because of the ice storm, it was impossible for us to leave Clarks Summit and travel the two hundred miles west to get to the hospital at Olean, so we dedicated the night to calling out to God from our room there at Clarks Summit and got up very early the next morning to cautiously start the trip west. By a little after noon, we were at the hospital. Jeremy was doing somewhat better, but he had no short-term memory. He would constantly ask what time it was or what day it was. It was quite scary to see him in those conditions. There were many questions in our minds at that time about the future for our son who had been, up to that point, a straight-A student. We just had to leave it with the Lord.

The next day, I had to drive back to Clarks Summit as I was to speak at the closing service of the conference on Friday morning. On my way out of town, I stopped by the scene of the accident to see what I could see. As I looked through the pieces of glass and plastic strewn all over the area where the car had rolled and gone against a tree, I found a pencil on the ground. It was obviously a pencil that we had been given in one of the churches where we had recently ministered. The verse spoke of the absolute peace that we can have as we trust in God our refuge. I bowed my head and thanked God for His watch-care over Jeremy, and knew that as I drove back to Clarks Summit to minister, I could trust Him for His best in Jeremy's life.

Back in Italy, the TV programs went out regularly by means of the video tapes that I had delivered to the stations prior to our departure. Radio Luce stayed on the air in spite of a fire one night (an electric blanket that short circuited—miraculously, while bed-ridden Maria Luisa, sick with the flu, had gotten up during the night to go into the bathroom).

During the summer of our furlough, we reported on our ministry in the Summit Baptist Bible Church that had supported us since 1971. After the Sunday morning service, we were invited to the Ransom home for dinner. After dinner as we sat and talked with Mark and Shirley (the children had all gone outside to play), they told us about their son, Daniel, who had just graduated from high school. Before going off to a secular college to study broadcasting, they really wanted him to have an opportunity to work for three months at a Christian radio station—like Radio Luce. Would we be willing to bring him in as a guest in our home for a three-month stay?

We were leaving our first son in America, and we thought that filling his spot at the table might be a good thing for all of us. We did need a lot of help with the radio. Daniel was obviously a young man who was very involved in operating the sound system at the church and thus had some experience, so we said "yes".

Shortly before our return to Italy, the Ransoms called to let us know that Daniel's round-trip airline ticket for three months would cost as much as one for a year. Would we be willing to have him stay with us for a year? We did need the help and committed to keeping him for a year.

It was wonderful to see how Daniel became a member of the family. He did a couple of months of language school and then became fluent spending time with Italians. After a few months in Italy, he asked me if he could do a live program on the radio. Why not? He soon became as at home behind the microphone in Italian as he had already been in English.

CHAPTER TWENTY-NINE

When a Short-Termer Becomes a Son, a Co-worker, and a Son-in-law
1997-2001

In the summer of 1997, Daniel went home to the States but, while there, realized that his place was in Italy, so he asked if he could come back for another year. Why not? He was already a vital part of our family as well as of the radio ministry here. He began analyzing our operations and came up with some wonderful renovations that are the core of our very professional radio outreach today. On the internet, he discovered a professional system for running our radio off the computer. From here, we moved on to downloading files, even hourly newscasts and weather reports, and finally streaming on the internet (www.radioluce.com).

While at a winter camp with our youth, God challenged Daniel to give his life for full-time service here in Italy. He also renewed his commitment to stay and help us out here in the ministry, even though he had no support. Daniel was soon able to get a job in a local television station, and then had some means of income. At a certain point, Daniel asked if he could take Elizabeth out for pizza. This was a moment of great joy for Elizabeth's parents. Where could Elizabeth ever find a better husband and partner in ministry than Daniel?

After several months of dating, the time was coming up for Elizabeth to go back to the States for college. Daniel felt that it was time for him to go as well so that they could do BBC together. Before leaving, they announced their intentions to marry and serve the Lord together. After a year and a half in separate dorms, they came back to Italy on Christmas break in December of 2003 to celebrate their marriage with their families, Italian friends, and believers in the Centro Evangelico Battista di San Sisto at Perugia's City Hall. Of course, the ceremony was followed by an Italian wedding feast! After a brief honeymoon in Sicily, they returned to Clarks Summit to resume classes and work. Elizabeth graduated in 2007 and Daniel in 2008. They then joined Baptist Mid-Missions for future ministry in Italy.

CHAPTER THIRTY

Extreme Trust
1998

In the summer of 1998, Rachel, Jonathan, and Elizabeth were in the States helping her parents while Jeremy, Joshua and I remained in Italy so that I could be with the church and the boys could work at McDonald's saving money for college. At the end of the summer, the boys went to a week of camp, and then we had our tickets to leave for the States to join the rest of the family, do a short furlough, get Jeremy set up at college, and then return to Italy.

In the middle of the camp week, I got a call from the camp nurse telling me that Jeremy had been taken to the hospital with severe stomach pain. When I arrived at the hospital in Teramo, they were waiting for my signature to perform emergency surgery for an obstructed intestine. The surgery went well, but now we were in a bind. Our non-refundable charter flight from Rome to New York was scheduled to leave the next morning, several days before the doctors would be ready to let Jeremy leave the hospital. I spoke with a friend who was a nurse at the hospital and explained to him our dilemma. He assured me that Jeremy was not in a life-threatening situation, and if he was in our situation, he would sign him out and take him to the airport for the flight.

With those encouraging words, I drove the four-hour trip back to Perugia and, with Josh's help, packed Jeremy for college.

Later that evening, we picked up Jeremy's girlfriend Francesca, who was going to the States with us, and made the trip back to Teramo. We arrived at the hospital at about 12:30 in the morning. I signed Jeremy out, and the nurse unhooked his I.V. He left the drainage bag hooked up so that Jeremy would be more comfortable on the trip. We made Jeremy as comfortable as we could in the back seat of the van, and by 1:00, we were on our way to Rome, about four hours away, to be able to catch our 7:00 A.M. flight to the States with not a minute to spare.

When we arrived at the ring road around Rome, we found a huge traffic jam, and it would be impossible for us to make it to the airport in time. Fabio, the Italian friend who was going to take our van home for us, held a handkerchief out the window while we moved up the emergency lane. By about 5:30, we were at the airport, and after getting a wheelchair for Jeremy, we got all checked in.

The flight left on time, and we all breathed a sigh of relief. Jeremy was not well or comfortable in the wheelchair, but under the circumstances, we could not ask for more. After about an hour in the air, we noticed that his drainage bag had puffed up, and that scared us. I asked the stewardess if she could ask over the intercom if there was a doctor on board. There was, and he kindly looked at Jeremy, and, after expressing concern over the fact that we had taken him out of the hospital under those conditions, he assured us that it was normal for that sack to inflate while airborne and that Jeremy would be all right.

When we arrived at JFK Airport, Rachel, Jonathan, and Elizabeth were waiting for us along with my folks who had driven them down to New York. As we came out with our luggage, she saw me but didn't recognize the person I was pushing in the wheelchair! It was her second son!

After nearly a four-hour trip to Latham, we got Jeremy to bed, and the next day, we were able to get him to a surgeon to continue his post-operative care and monitor his recovery. After a week of camping in the mountains, we were on our way to take him to college. God gave him a remarkable recovery.

Jeremy's first day on campus, before he was even enrolled, he had been hired by food service where he worked for all three years at the college.

CHAPTER THIRTY-ONE

How to Share the Story –
The First Italian Christian History Tour
1999

(Tour hosts Dr. Carter and Fred)

Over the course of nearly thirty years after our graduation from Baptist Bible College of Pennsylvania, Dr. Rembert Carter and I had shared a dream—a Christian History Tour in Italy. How else could we get supporters from the States to come over and experience the ministry in Italy? A tour seemed to be just the ticket. The Lord provided a reputable tour company in Italy, and in 1999, "The Italian Christian History Tour" became a reality thanks to the help of my parents, George and Jean Whitman, who advertised, collected the money, and arranged the flights for those who would be part of the first tour. As we visited Rome, Assisi, Perugia, Siena, Florence, Pisa, the Waldensian Valleys, Venice, Trent, and Pompeii, we learned about God's outworking of history on Italian soil. Of course, the weekend involved worshipping alongside the Italian believers at the Centro Evangelico Battista started by us back in 1976.

As the tour wound down, in a final group meeting, I asked the folks to share the most exciting thing they had witnessed in Italy. Having taken them to the Coliseum, the Catacombs, the Sistine Chapel, Pompeii, and Florence's Uffizi Galleries, to name a few, you can imagine my joy when almost all of them said that their favorite thing was the Sunday with our church! Praise the Lord. An audio-video summary of this trip is available on a DVD.

A special treat on that first tour, Dr. and Mrs. Carter's first visit to Italy, was the surprise arrival of Gretchen, their daughter, who was teaching M.K.s in Norway at the time but was able to participate in the tour. Those former Western Civ. students who had studied under Dr. Carter could just close their eyes on those bus trips and reminisce of those bygone days at BBC while they traveled over the highways of Italy. By the time we organized the second tour, Dr. Carter was ill, and by the time of the third, he was with the Lord. Those tours, with the participation of several from our supporting churches as well as my parents all three times, are some of our greatest memories in all these years.

(Tour group in Pompeii)

(Tour guide in Venice)

CHAPTER THIRTY-TWO

A World-Class Soccer Star in Our Little Church
2000

In late summer of 2000, I found several phone messages in which a foreigner was trying to get information about our services. We played phone tag for a several days, and finally I was home when Marcelo called. He told me his name, but it didn't ring a bell. He explained that he and his family had recently accepted Christ in Brazil, but now they were living in

Perugia. They had seen my Gospel program on television and would like to fellowship with our church. Hearing the foreign accent, I asked him if he was a student in Perugia. He replied, "No, my name is Zé Maria, and I play in the Perugia Soccer Club." He wanted to meet me and invited me to come to the TV station that night where he was doing an interview on a sports show.

As I walked into the studio, the show host recognized me. My program had been on television for the last twenty-one years. He asked me to come on camera, and they gave me a seat next to Zé Maria, who proceeded to present me to the viewing audience as "his pastor." Only during that telecast did I start to understand who Zé Maria was. In addition to starring on several Brazilian teams, he had also played over forty games with the Brazil *national* soccer team. He had also played on teams for Parma and Perugia in Italy's A-league prior to an injury that had threatened to end his career at its height.

As the sports doctor tried to cure his ailments, he came to the place of telling Marcelo that he would no longer treat him as Zé Maria, the soccer star, but as Marcelo, who would no longer be playing soccer. After that news, Marcelo went home and in tears told his wife Sandra the bad news. In desperation, they called Sandra's mom in Brazil. Unbeknownst to them, Sandra's mom had recently come to know Christ and His forgiveness in her life. She responded to their desperation with hope. She said, "I am a follower of Jesus now, and we will pray for you at the church. If it is God's will, you will play soccer again; if not, He will provide for you if you trust Him."

The next week, Marcelo went back to the doctor for a follow-up visit. After examining Marcelo for some time, he said, "Now, what was your problem? I can find nothing!" God had answered the prayers of the believers in that Brazilian Baptist Church, and Marcelo was healed!

The family left Perugia and returned home to Brazil. They all started attending the church that had prayed for them. In time, the entire family professed Christ as Savior and was baptized, becoming members of the local church. Meanwhile, Marcelo played a year of soccer on two clubs in the São Paulo area before being invited to return to Perugia. At that point in their lives, the Lord brought us together thanks to the television outreach.

For four years, Zé Maria played for Perugia, as they were in the Italian A-league, and used his notoriety as a soccer celebrity to get the Gospel out in as many ways as possible. On several occasions, we had special outreaches, and many unsaved men visited the church and heard the Gospel for the first time. In those years, several of his teammates came with him to visit the church, one of whom won the 2006 World Cup for Italy with his penalty kick. I met with Marcelo regularly for prayer on Saturday morning as the team would leave for their pre-game retreat, usually in front of the bus as they awaited their departure. Of course, it was impossible for him to be in church on most Sundays.

I still remember the first time the family came to the church. It was the Wednesday evening after we first met. I hadn't mentioned to anyone about him coming because he was such a famous soccer star; I didn't want people showing up just to see him. As it was, from that time on, very often on Sundays that the team didn't have a game and it was possible for him to worship with us, there were journalists and dads with their sons who waited outside the church to get an interview or a signature. One young man, Vincenzo, actually came to the church to see Zé Maria and ended up getting saved, baptized, and added to the church.

CHAPTER THIRTY-THREE

Our First Wedding in the Family
2001

Jeremy and Francesca had known each other since they were very young. Her family attended our church before she started school. In fact, Francesca's older brother Simone was Jeremy's best friend throughout the elementary school years. We had known her parents since before they were married. After years of growing up together in church and sharing summer camp experiences and youth group, as Jeremy was nearing his time to return to the States for college, a match was lit. Their trans-Atlantic relationship grew during the years of college, and after Jeremy's graduation from Cornerstone College, it was time to take the step.

July 7th was a beautiful day in central Italy. Many dear friends and family members had flown in from the States. Francesca was a beautiful bride as she came down the aisle of Perugia's thirteenth-century City Hall to the sound of a brass choir. After the legal aspect was cared for by the mayor's representative, Jeremy's grandfather Whitman and dad officiated in the service. After the recessional and pictures, the guests gathered at a local restaurant for a lovely Italian feast. After their honeymoon, they left for the States where Jeremy would do his graduate studies at Grand Valley in Grand Rapids.

CHAPTER THIRTY-FOUR

That Little Italian Evangelist –
John Carrara
2001

For many years, my dad had told me of an elderly Italian evangelist (my dad had heard him preach shortly after his conversion in the late '30s) who really wanted to come to Italy and preach. Although Dr. Carrara had had a very successful ministry in America with thousands of souls saved over a seventy-year ministry, having never met him and knowing that he didn't speak Italian, I had some doubts as to how effective his ministry could be in Italy.

After months of planning and praying, Dr. Carrara, eighty-eight years of age, was on his way to the airport on September 11th, 2001 when, because of the terrorist attack on the twin towers and the Pentagon, his flight was canceled. We were able to reschedule him in November of that year. His testimony of faith in Christ really moved our folk. Dr. John was saved out of a Roman Catholic background and severely persecuted for his faith by his family and priest. In the early '20s, he had experienced many things in his Roman Catholic neighborhood in Fairfield, New Jersey, that our folks had experienced in their more recent lifetimes on Italian soil.

Many unsaved people came out to the meetings and heard the Gospel for the first time. Several were saved. Our folks were so excited about the ministry of this little Italian "nonno" that Dr. Carrara came over for six consecutive years. On his last visit, he was soon to turn ninety-four, and he told me that most likely that would be his last ministry with us. The next year, he took sick and soon after went to be with the Lord. Our loss is Heaven's gain! Our church was greatly blessed by his ministry. Nearly every visit, the Lord brought new people to Himself.

Dr. John's love for our church was shown even after his "home-going" too. Our church family was moved to tears at the news that in his last will and testament, he had left a substantial amount of money to help us in our church renovation project! Thank You, Lord, and thank you, Dr. John!

(Fred interpreting for John Carrara)

CHAPTER THIRTY-FIVE

Three Weddings in a Year and an Empty Nest
2002-2003

For the Christmas holidays of 2002, all of our children came back from the States. We were getting geared up for our second wedding in the family. Josh and Sara decided that they couldn't live another year apart, her in Bologna and him in college in Grand Rapids.

They had met at a Bible Institute in the mountains of central Italy. Josh introduced Sara to me telling me that they were reading the Bible together. I could see the handwriting on the wall. Their desire to serve the Lord together grew into a serious relationship. This brought them through several years of separation with Joshua in America for his studies.

The day before the wedding, we all drove to Bologna to help get ready for the big day. Once again, many fine friends arrived from the States to help us celebrate. We gathered at the bride's home for breakfast on that crisp January morning and then dressed up and headed toward the church building in the historic center of Bologna. The ceremony was conducted by the pastor of Sara's church, one of very few Gospel-preaching churches in the entire city of Bologna. Afterwards, all the invited guests went to a lovely restaurant for the wedding dinner which went on until late in the evening. The newlyweds left for their honeymoon, and the Whitmans left for the three-hour trip back to Perugia for their Sunday services the next morning.

In August, Rachel and I joined the rest of the family that were already in the States for their studies for Jonathan and Melodee's wedding. Rachel had gone early to help in the preparations, and I had to come later because of my obligations in the ministry in Italy. My job in coming later was to bring several pounds of fresh mozzarella cheese in my hand baggage so that Rachel would have the proper fixings for the lasagna that she would be making for family and wedding party dinner the night before the wedding.

The next morning, we gathered with much of our family and several hundred guests and well-wishers at the Calvary Baptist Church that had been Jonathan and Melodee's home church during their college years. It also became their commissioning church when they returned to Italy as missionaries.

The ceremony was officiated by Rev. Jeff Zimmerman, Melodee's dad, Rev. George P. Whitman, Jonathan's grandfather, and myself. After the wedding, the newlyweds left for their honeymoon, and shortly thereafter, Rachel and I returned to the ministry in Italy.

As the Christmas holidays approached later that year, Jonathan, Jeremy, Joshua, and their wives all came back to Italy along with Daniel's family and several friends to participate in Daniel and Elizabeth's wedding. Since our entire family had been in the States, we had suggested to Elizabeth that they get married over there. The bride-to-be replied that she was going to have an Italian dinner at her wedding, and she wanted her church family in Italy to be there to celebrate with her and Daniel.

Once again, we were able to have the ceremony in Perugia's thirteenth-century City Hall. It was a lovely cold and sunny day in Perugia. The bride came down the aisle accompanied by her dad (me) to the lovely strains of a string quartet played by

Elizabeth's friends from the music conservatory. The ceremony was officiated by Rev. Mark Ransom, Daniel's dad, and myself. The wedding dinner was held at the same lovely restaurant where Jeremy and Francesca's had been held several years earlier.

Daniel and Elizabeth left on their honeymoon, and all too soon, the other children returned to the States with their spouses, and Rachel and I were left with an empty nest, almost. We still had Julius Ceasar, Elizabeth's cat.

CHAPTER THIRTY-SIX

Exciting Testimonies
from Some of the Fruits of Our Labors

ESTER – "I came to Italy from Chile as a political refugee with my husband and two small boys. My husband was very abusive. Many times, he forced me to count out loud as he would strike me with each blow. Often, I passed out after counting up to 100. He also beat the children and actually left one of them with permanent damage to his arm."

"One day, when the boys were still quite small, he left me for another woman, and I had to find work to provide for them. During that time, I met an Italian man who, although he was a drug addict, invited me and my sons to live with him so that we would have a roof over our heads. More than once during the years that we lived together, he went into a coma from the heroin that he was shooting up with, but each time when they came to get him with the ambulance and treated him at the hospital, he somehow came out of it. One day in 1985, I had an aneurism on the brain and went into a coma. I was not expected to live, but miraculously, with a lot of treatment I came out of it and returned home to care for my boys. In the midst of my very sad and difficult life, I met a friend from Chile who invited me to come to church with her."

"This friend, Lucia, also had a very difficult marriage. In fact, the night that she was saved, she had been planning to stab her husband to death when he returned to the house. He had abandoned her for nearly two weeks, pregnant with a small child and no money to buy food or pay rent. One evening, she was invited to a Bible Study and, after hearing the Gospel, accepted Christ in her life as her Lord and Savior. After the meeting, she went home with her heart full of the joy of sins forgiven. The proof that she had truly come to know the forgiveness of Christ in her life was seen in the fact that she actually welcomed her husband home and forgave him for the evil way that he had treated her. When she invited me to visit her church, I was hoping for a miracle in my life too. I started attending the monthly church dinners, arriving after the worship time. I did feel guilty doing this, so I soon started attending the Tuesday Ladies' Bible Study. That afternoon, I invited the Pastor (Fred Whitman) to come for a visit."

"That evening, March 19, 1987, Pastor Whitman came to our little apartment to talk, and he explained the Gospel to us. As I sat at the table beside Tiziano, who I was living with, as well as a friend of his who was also involved in drugs and another friend of mine, I listened to the Gospel story. God opened my heart to understand that Jesus had died in my place. I understood for the first time my need of Him as my Savior and Lord, and I prayed, asking Him to forgive me and come into my life. He did! It didn't bother me that neither my boyfriend nor his friend was interested. I had decided to follow Jesus with my life, regardless of the cost. 'He that taketh not his cross and followeth after me, is not worthy of me. He that findeth his life shall lose it: and he that loseth his life for my sake shall find it.

He that receiveth you receiveth me, and he that receiveth me receiveth him that sent me.' Matthew 10:39-40."

"I felt so light. My burdens were lifted. Even though today I have some physical problems, since I came to know Christ, every day is a miracle for me. Jesus is my Doctor, my Savior, and my Comforter. If He hadn't come along beside me, I would have tried to take my life many times. The Lord is now forever beside me and has given me the certainty of eternal life. I know that I will live with Him forever—without illnesses or problems—because He had mercy toward me and saved me. For this I daily thank Him as well as for the husband that He put beside me who now loves the Lord and takes care of me. Now I'll let my husband Tiziano tell his side of the story."

TIZIANO – "After growing up on the streets of Rome in drugs and especially heroin for about twenty years, my family moved back to Perugia, where I had been born, in an attempt to get me out of drugs. It didn't work. I easily found them in Perugia too. My girlfriend Ester had a brain aneurism, and during that crisis, I prayed for the first time, selfishly asking God to spare her life. He did answer my prayer to spare her life, but that didn't change the way that I was living. I just got deeper and deeper into drugs, even stealing from my parents and robbing strangers to pay for my habit."

"After Pastor Whitman's visit at our apartment that night, my girlfriend's life was radically changed. Pastor Whitman, who I had seen years earlier in Rome on his Gospel telecast 'La Bibbia Oggi', did his best to get me to visit the church with Ester, but it was too convenient for me to drop her off on Sunday and then go and buy my drug supply for the week. One day after church, as I stopped in front of the church to pick up Ester, Pastor Whitman came out to greet me. He asked me if I was afraid to visit the church, and I assured him that I wasn't. In fact, the next Sunday morning, I came to church with Ester. I was given a Bible and challenged to begin reading it."

"One Friday evening as I read about how the Lord Jesus had suffered on the cross, I understood that He had done it for me. My wrecked life and my slavery to drugs had become unsupportable. I cried out to God for His help, believing His promise, 'Believe on the Lord Jesus Christ and you will be saved.' I had already set up an appointment for the next morning to drive a friend of mine to pick up our drugs for the week. I kept my promise and drove for him, but I didn't buy any for myself. In fact, from that night I never touched heroin again! Praise the Lord!"

"After I accepted the Lord Jesus Christ into my life, Pastor Fred told me that if I really wanted to be serious about being a disciple of Christ, I would need to interrupt my adulterous relationship and move out of my house, leaving Ester and her boys to sleep there alone. He offered me a bed at his house in his boys' room, and I went there to live for several months until Ester and I were able to get married. Over these past twenty years, I have had my ups and downs, but I know that the Lord has saved me, changed my life, and will carry me ahead until He comes for me."

"As I look back over these years of the Lord's faithfulness, I especially remember a wonderful way that the Lord used me for His glory. After I was saved, I had a burden to reach my former drug-friends with the Gospel. Two of these, Ivano and Massimo, in consequence of their sharing of needles had contracted AIDS. As I would go to visit them, they would try (unsuccessfully) to get me to smoke pot with them. They were also very angry that I, who had shared their needles, miraculously had not been infected with AIDS as they had been. Even though they made fun of me, I kept returning to talk with them and talk to them about Jesus, what He had done for me and what he could do for them."

"One night, Ivano, who at this point was totally bed-ridden, prayed and put his trust in the Lord Jesus Christ. He was miraculously changed. Instead of cursing God's name and swearing, he wanted me to pray and read the Bible with him. The next day, I took Pastor Fred to visit him, and he said that it was one of the most glorious conversions that he had ever seen. One month exactly after Ivano found pardon and forgiveness in the Lord, he was taken into His presence, never to suffer again. I am so glad that I'll see him in heaven, even though his brother Massimo, rejected the Lord until the end."

VILLELMA – "I was raised on a farm in the country shortly after World War I. We were so poor that all of the children had to work in the fields. I was only able to go to school for part of my first year of elementary school and then had to go to work with my brothers and sisters. Our family was very religious, and we were brought up to be very faithful Catholics. However, as a young lady, I married a man who did not believe in God and was against my religious zeal. He didn't like me going to Mass every day, often very early in the morning."

"For myself, in spite of my religion, I did not have peace with God and sought to fill the void in my life. One day, as I shopped at the open market, a physically handicapped man who I had often seen begging offered me a small Gospel tract. As I read it after returning home, I noticed that it offered a free Bible study. My son helped me fill out the coupon, and I sent it in. After receiving the study in the mail, my young son helped me read it, and I put my trust in Christ as my Savior. Sometime later, I was visited by some believers from a small evangelical church and was baptized. When Fred and Rachel Whitman began their ministry in my town, I was encouraged to join in their ministry where I have been faithful since 1975."

"Over the years, I have suffered much for my faith, but God has been faithful. My late husband beat me many times and tore my Bible to pieces if I forgot and left it out where he could find it. I now have not only children but grandchildren and great-grandchildren, but in all these years, I have not had the joy of seeing any of them come to the faith. That would be my greatest desire, to see even one person in my family get saved before I go to be with the Lord."

MARIA – "I was raised in a working-class family and very early got a job in the Perugina Candy Factory at Perugia. I married a man who was Communist. Having been raised (and sexually abused) by the nuns in an orphanage, he hated God and everything that represented Him or religion. Through the testimony of an elderly Christian lady, I put my faith in Christ, and when the Whitmans opened the Centro Evangelico Battista in 1976 at San Sisto, I began attending there. I was baptized the same time as their oldest son Jonathan in 1983 and have been faithful to the Lord in the church ever since, although neither my husband nor my daughters and their families have trusted Christ as their Savior as of yet."

DONATELLA – "I was raised in a very hard-working, nominally Catholic family. From my early teen years, I worked in our family pastry shop each day while carrying on my studies. I graduated from the University of Perugia with a degree in philosophy. All my life, I struggled with depression, striving to reach up to the expectations of my workaholic parents. The first thirty-five years of my life I spent searching for a truth that would give me happiness. I searched in materialism, in hard work, and in the search of intellectual knowledge, but nothing in all of this filled my void of happiness."

"I was unsatisfied, and this brought me to my depression. I spent a lot of time in which I was not able to dominate my mind but I was dominated by it. I could no longer live without tranquilizers. The hours of my day were taken up by alternating anxiety and anguish. One day, while in the throes of a deep depression, under doctor's care and medication, I met an American missionary wife whose daughter was in the same class of elementary school as my daughter. As we talked of my problems, she told me that the final solution to my problem was in a book, the Bible, in which I would find the only Doctor who could cure me, Jesus Christ. She gave me a Bible, but I was too busy with family and work to do much serious reading."

"One day, I fell and broke my leg. I was laid up for several weeks. In that time, I began reading the Bible she had given me, together with the Catholic Bible. We had been taught that the Protestants believed differently than we did because their Bible had been falsified. As I read the two Bibles side by side, I discovered that the text of both Bibles was very similar. The difference was that often the explanation at the bottom of the page in the Catholic Bible had nothing to do with the plain meaning that was obvious in both of the texts."

"At a certain point as I read the Scriptures, I came to realize that Jesus had died in my place and I needed to put my whole soul trust in His death for me on the cross. It was not a change of religion. It was a total change in my life. That was in 1990. When it came time for my baptism, I was still working every day at our family pastry shop. Many Sundays, in order to be able to fellowship and worship at the church, I would go to work at 3:00 A.M so that I could leave from 9:00 A.M. until noon to fellowship with my fellow believers and sit under the preaching of the Word, to then return to work for the afternoon. I thank the Lord for His faithfulness in my life, even though after all these years, my husband has still not understood the grace of God in salvation revealed in the Lord Jesus Christ."

"I praise the Lord for my depression and for my encounter with one of His servants because, from that time, I started to search for the answers in the right place. I discovered day by day in the pages of His Word and with the help of His church my lost condition, the reasons for my dissatisfaction, and my absolute need of someone who could take away my sins. The Holy Spirit convinced my heart of my lost condition as a sinner and brought my feet to the cross. He put in my hand the hammer and the nails, telling me that I was there that day beating Jesus and nailing Him to the cross with my sins. The words of Romans 8:15 resounded in my mind giving me in that moment the certainty and the peace to be a child of God, forgiven by means of the sacrifice of my Savior. Today, after eighteen years, I can cry out to the world that in the Bible I found the healing for my depression, and in Jesus Christ I found the Doctor who healed my soul for eternity. My thanks to You, My Lord and My Savior!"

LUCA – "I am Donatella's son. I thank the Lord that while I was very young, my parents began attending the Centro Evangelico Battista and I grew up under the teaching of the Word. As a child, I suffered from severe dyslexia and was often placed in the corner of the classroom and left to myself, as they thought that I had severe mental problems. During that time period, Rachel Whitman, my pastor's wife, attended a master's class in dyslexia. After her course, she was able to help me greatly in overcoming my problem. I was able to get a diploma from a trade school and am now a professional electrician. I accepted Christ at 10 years of age and was later baptized."

"During my late teen years, I had a girlfriend who wasn't a Christian. Through the counsel of Jonathan Whitman, I realized that if I was going to be a faithful disciple of the Lord Jesus, I could not be "unequally yoked" and I had to break off our relationship. It was very difficult for me, but the Lord gave me grace. About a year later, I heard that she had accepted Christ as Savior and Lord, and sometime later, I got in contact with her again. We are now engaged and are waiting on the Lord for His perfect timing to be united in marriage so as to serve the Lord together with our lives."

VINCENZO – "I was born and raised in Naples in a working-class family. In 2000, because of the need of employment, my family moved up to Perugia. At that point in my life, my god was soccer, and my goal in life was to become a professional soccer player. I played on several youth league teams and excelled. Sometime after we moved to Perugia, I heard that Marcelo Zé Maria, a former star of the Brazilian National Soccer team who now was playing on the Perugia team, was now attending the Centro Evangelico Battista! I started going to that church hoping to get to know him and possibly get some help from him in my soccer career. The day I came to church, Marcelo gave his testimony of how he had come to put his trust in the Lord Jesus as his personal Savior. As I began attending the church, sometime later, I realized that I also needed to ask the Lord's forgiveness and trust Him as my Personal Savior. I was baptized several years later, and I am now one of the leaders in the youth group, helping out in a weekly radio program on Radio Luce called 'Sky Zone'. My goal is to attend a Bible College in America to prepare for the Lord's service as I believe that someday the Lord wants to use me in a youth ministry."

RAFFAELE – "My testimony of faith to have accepted Jesus as my personal Savior is the following: It came about at the time when I was seriously injured at work. In that moment, all of my past life passed before me, and I understood that without the Lord, all my life was worth nothing. During the time that I was in the hospital, I placed myself in His hands, asking Him forgiveness for my sins. I was really scared because of the operations that I had to have, but Jesus was at my side consoling and protecting me. Only in this way I could feel some of the suffering as I imagined that the Lord had endured on the cross for me and for the world."

"Many were surprised at my reaction to my injury because instead of drawing away from God and being angry with Him, I came closer to Him, desiring more and more to serve Him with my whole life. I believe that it was for me a great trial of my faith, which I overcame with His help. I meditate much on His Word and pray that He will give me the ability and the wisdom to bring to many people the knowledge of the truth because Jesus is the truth. Let this be my testimony for someone that in this moment is reading my story and is in the condition that I was before I came to know Christ."

"I am Vincenzo's uncle. My family also moved up to Perugia from Naples to seek work. Shortly after moving to Perugia, my wife met Donatella in a store and found out that she was an evangelical Christian. She invited us to the Centro Evangelico Battista, and my wife began attending some with our three children. Unfortunately, for various reasons, one of which was her work schedule, this did not continue for very long."

"Meanwhile, I was too busy with work to think about going to church on Sunday. I had to be away from the family all week for work, and when I was home on the weekends I had too much to do to be able to put church in my schedule. That was my past life."

"I feel privileged to have had the trial of my faith, like Job did, as well as other men of God in the past. What counts is not the body but the spirit and soul which will go to be with God. One day at the work site, I was involved in a serious accident in which I lost the fourth toe of my left foot, but that doesn't matter to me. I am happy, very happy because God is with me. I would also like to thank my pastor, Fred. During my trials, he and Jonathan, his son were always near me, giving me Biblical teaching."

"During my time of suffering and mental anguish in the hospital, realizing that I might not ever be able to work again and support my family, I called out in desperation to the Lord. I know that he heard my cry and as I trusted Him with my life I came to realize His forgiveness and His promise to never leave me or forsake me. Thank you, thank you to those who help our church financially as well as all of God's missionaries. Above all, thanks to God for what He is doing in my life."

"I have now been baptized and become a member of the church (Centro Evangelico Battista) and am anxious to serve the Lord in any way that He would see fit. I would really like to study the Word of God and someday learn how to preach and teach it for the glory of God. Meanwhile, my family has taken a step back from their interest in spiritual things, and I pray that soon they will be able to share with me my enthusiasm in living for and in serving the Lord in the local church."

MARIO – "I was raised in a normal Italian Catholic family, and my studies brought me a degree in mechanical engineering.

As a young man, I was engaged and married; however, I found out shortly thereafter that my bride had cheated on me the night before our wedding with her former boyfriend, and very soon, after a short time of marriage, she left me for him. After years of spiritual crisis, I met a young lady who told me about Jesus and His power to save and forgive. Sometime later, I was baptized and joined the church. Several years later, we were married and have founded our home on the Word of God. It is a joy to walk together as a couple in the light of the Word of God in obedience to his Commandments, seeking to please Him and serve Him with our lives."

SENIJA – "I was born in Sarajevo, Yugoslavia, in a Muslim family. When I was four and my sister two, we moved to Italy because my mom had cancer. It was wartime in Yugoslavia, and the hospitals had no anesthesia. My mom had already been operated on once without anesthesia, and my dad was not going to let her go through that again. We came to Perugia because there was a good cancer clinic."

"After three years of treatment, my mom died. During this time, my Dad, who in Yugoslavia was a music teacher, had to get a job mixing cement at a construction site. After my mom's death, we moved about a half hour away from Perugia to a little town called Magione. There, I met a lot of new friends. My dad also got a girlfriend. One day, one of my friends was visiting our apartment while Patrizia, my dad's girlfriend, was watching

Pastor Fred's TV program, 'La Bibbia Oggi'. My friend exclaimed, 'That is our pastor! We go to church at the Centro Evangelico Battista!' She then invited us to go with her to their youth group on Friday night. We then began going on Sundays too."

"After several weeks of attending the church, I came to realize my need of the Lord Jesus as my personal Savior and put my trust in Him. Several months later, I was baptized and joined the church. During those months, my dad, who was Muslim, came to church with us. One Sunday, as Pastor Fred was finishing the message, my Dad, to my surprise, stood to his feet and said, 'Pastor, may I say something?' He then added, 'Many of you know that I am a Muslim. What you don't know is that in these months, I have come to realize that there is salvation only in Jesus, and I have put my trust in Him.' There was not a dry eye in our tiny church! Pray for my dad that he'll go ahead with the Lord and grow in His grace and knowledge. Meanwhile, Patrizia has accepted Christ as her Savior, and they have been married. My sister, sadly, has not gone ahead with the Lord as of the present moment."

GALIA – "I was raised in Moldavia, which at that time was part of the Soviet Union. My family was Russian Orthodox, and we were very religious. It has now been over five years since I came to know the Lord. As a young child, I believed that perhaps there was a God who protected me, but I was never sure. When I was six years old, my mom died, so my spiritual education was taken over by my grandparents. Since they were very religious, they often took me to the worship service at the Orthodox Church. From that time, I began attending either the Orthodox or Catholic church."

"At twenty years of age, I was married, and everything seemed to be going well. Inside of me, however, I felt a great void. Later, in tragic circumstances, my dear brother died. I was very close to him. From that time on the thought of death terrorized me."

"After several other situations, I finally arrived in Italy. I was very bitter because I had family problems, problems at home and at work. I was very homesick for my daughter who I had left in Moldavia when I came to Italy to find work. One day, I met Silvia, who now is a dear sister in the faith. She began to speak to me about the Lord. She told me that there was a solution for my problems, and so I began to do a Bible study with her. God spoke to me by means of that Bible study, and I understood my sinful condition, but I was not ready yet to open my heart to Him. I then learned about the Centro Evangelico Battista and began to go there to church on Sunday mornings. There were special meetings with evangelist John Carrara, and at one of those services, November 3, 2002, having heard the message on John 6:35-37, I opened my heart to the Lord Jesus. He became my personal Savior, and the emptiness in my heart was filled. Later several brothers and sisters in Christ came around me, and we prayed together. From that moment I feel like I am part of a great family."

"On June 23, 2005, I was baptized and joined the Baptist Church. I continue to go forward, walking with the Lord and serving Him the best I can. My daughter, Sabrina, has also been saved and baptized and is now a very active part of the youth ministry of the Centro Evangelico Battista. Praise the Lord!"

ANNA – "I was raised in southern Italy, near Foggia. For my work, I was transferred to Modena and then Perugia. In those years, I suffered greatly with depression. I now can give an answer to so many questions in my past life. I now know exactly what happened to me one day while crying in my kitchen, as I listened to the radio in order to be distracted from my desperation. Now I know that Jesus was waiting for me with open arms, and my tears would have been dried up in his handkerchief of love. This is how I came to know the Lord, that day when the frequency of the radio, "by chance" (I know that it wasn't by chance), tuned in to Radio Luce."

"My life was finished; I was at a crossroads, I did not love my husband any more or even the persons that were around me. I didn't even love myself any more. I wanted a new life since mine was now destroyed in the desires of thousands of useless things and in the separation from my husband, the man that God had given me. Listening to Maria Luisa on the radio, as she spoke of the Psalms, I saw myself, I saw once again my life, and I decided that day to contact the Centro Evangelico Battista. Thank the Lord that I was able to. It was near the end of 2003. I began coming to a small Bible study on Tuesday with the ladies, finding there what I was looking for."

"The real change, however, the important moment that I remember in my heart, was when Dr. John Carrara had come to Italy for one of his ministry trips. It was October of 2005, and at the end of the service, he would ask if there was someone who was ready to accept Christ as Savior and Lord. One of those evenings, exactly October 13, 2005, my heart was broken. Inside me, I heard a voice that said, 'What? After all that I gave you and helped you see, you still don't want to come to me?' I remember still with great emotion that I raised my hand, and I thank the Lord that He called me to Himself. Now I am saved. I am His child. I love His Word with all my heart. My life has a fragrance of fresh air, and I will never have enough time to say enough times, 'Thank You, Lord.' I now have a daily program on Radio Luce. I am 53 years old, have two sons, Massimo (25) and Marco (21). Last year, the Lord called my husband Nicola to salvation. There could not be a greater joy in my life than that, and I am trusting the Lord that He'll also save my sons and the rest of my extended family."

ZOILA – "I am from Ecuador and am 36 years old. I am married and have a daughter that is 14 years of age."

"From when I was very young, my parents attended a small evangelical church, and I went with them. I can still remember a picture that hung in the back of the church, where there were two roads. One was a wide one in which the people prayed in front of a statue and men carried bottles of alcohol in their hands showing that they were alcoholics. The other road was a narrow one which lead to a house on which there was a sign, 'Evangelical Church.' I felt quite at peace with myself because I thought that by attending that church I was saved, but with the passing of time, listening to the messages of the pastor, I realized that it wasn't enough to just listen in order to be saved and to have eternal life."

"One of the verses that remained impressed on my mind after a summer camp that I attended is found in Psalm 119:11: 'Thy word have I hid in my heart that I might not sin against thee.' I repeated it often from memory. After several years, I realized that I was not respecting or obeying the Word of God, and I finally understood that I was a sinner who was falling deeper and deeper into the worst sins. At that point, I asked God for His forgiveness through Jesus Christ, His Son, and I accepted Him as my Lord. In September, a year after my daughter was born out of wedlock, I was baptized."

"In 1997, I arrived in Italy. I searched for a church in which to worship. I searched on the radio dial, and I found Radio Luce. I thank God that through the radio, He brought me to the Centro Evangelico Battista in 1998 because in this church, I understood how a true child of God needs to live."

"On September 3, 2006, after a message by Dr. John Carrara, I humbled myself before God because I realized that I was a baby believer who was not growing in spiritual things. Before the message, Becki, Pastor Fred's sister, sang 'To Your Name', and all the words of that song and of the message to follow touched my heart. Immediately in prayer, I asked the Lord to forgive my shortcoming before Him and to help me to grow every day and become a believer as He would desire."

"Now, I thank my Savior for His patience, mercy, and His infinite love that He has toward me. I know for sure that I do not deserve His Grace. Now, He has placed on my heart to continue in my obedience, to serve Him, praise Him, and thank Him for everything that He does, because I know that nothing happens by chance. Everything is in God's plans, and I am only an instrument in His hands, and I am just a part of His many projects. I am now married to the father of my daughter, and as he faithfully attends church with my daughter and me, it is my prayers that he too will soon understand salvation by grace through faith in the Lord Jesus Christ."

JENNIFER – "I was born into a family that already attended our church, so I always had the habit of going to church. Every Sunday we would go. I went to Sunday School, and my parents listened to the messages. For me, this meant 'knowing God'. In 2000, I began to realize that in reality, I did not have Jesus in my heart… because I had never given him the permission to enter. I had never prayed asking Him to enter my life! So one afternoon of November, I went to my mom and asked her some questions about Jesus. She gave me all the answers, and at the end asked me if I wanted to ask Jesus to enter my life. I immediately said 'Yes!' and we prayed together."

"A few days later, I went to church with Mom again to listen to the preaching of Dr. John Carrara who was on a preaching tour in Italy in that time period. That day, he gave his testimony of faith, a very moving story! He had to suffer to be able to live his life for God, and I wanted to do the same thing. When he finished preaching, he asked if there was anyone who had not yet accepted Christ as Savior. I went forward in tears to tell everyone that I also had a new heart. We then prayed together."

"From that moment, I began to really be interested in God's story. If first I went to church only to draw pictures and listen to a story, now I went to church to hear the true story of the life of my Savior!"

"In the summer, I began to attend the camp at Isola. I fell in love with that place. Because there I could meet many brothers and sisters in Christ, meet new people, and especially learn to know God better. I was very happy there."

"During my Jr. High School, I was the only girl in my class, except those who were Muslim, to not participate in religious instruction (only Roman Catholicism is taught). My friends were all curious about the fact that I was not in religion class, and it gave me the opportunity to explain that I was different because I truly believed in God. In reality, the only thing that my friends were interested in was that I could miss an hour of school and therefore I was 'lucky'."

"I then arrived at High School. I remember that the first day I was loaded down with all sorts of emotions. I was close to being overcome by my emotions, curiosity, shyness, and happiness. I had chosen the Classical High School, the school of my dreams. I was sure that I had made the right choice, except that the first day of school, I had to do go to the hospital and do some tests because I had felt sick the day before. I got out of the hospital after three months! Once I got home, I had to stay home for another week to avoid getting sick again. I did get better, and for this I thank the Lord. I also thank the Lord for my youth group who came to visit me regularly. I am also thankful for all the ones of my church who prayed regularly for me in that time."

"After this time, I returned to school, that school of my dreams in which I hoped to spend the five-year course developing wonderful friendships. It wasn't easy for me. I had to make up a lot of material in a very little time. I was always studying! I prayed God to help me avoid failing. He answered my prayer, and I passed!"

"However, I had come to realize that I couldn't continue in that school because I had missed out on too many of the foundations. My friends treated me as a stranger, and the professors didn't want to waste time explaining to me the lessons that I had missed. So I decided to go to a linguistic High School."

"As every story, mine has a beginning, a time of balance, and a time of great change that breaks the initial balance. The true change for me started in that summer because I became a little less timid, and I became more open with the people around me. This brought me problems because in my desire to have friends, I chose some who did not have a good influence in my life. I started going to the disco. The only person in the church that knew this tried to dissuade me from going, but I defined my wrong actions. I wasn't doing anything wrong."

"One night at the youth meeting, Jonathan couldn't be there to lead, so it was to be led by Vincenzo, Sabrina, and Senija. At the end, we got into a real discussion among the young people on wrong attitudes and actions. Someone brought up the subject of the disco. 'How can you go with all your good intentions when it is right there that Satan will attack you? And if Jesus came back while you were there? Would He be happy to find you there? I don't believe so.'"

"Hearing these words, I was petrified. I couldn't say anything. I couldn't look anyone in the face. I jumped up and ran into the bathroom, where I burst into tears. After a few seconds, Sabrina came into the bathroom. She had understood what was going on. I started telling her my story, telling her that I did not ever want to set foot in a disco again. I never wanted to commit that error again. So I asked forgiveness of the Lord, and we prayed together. Now I thank my mother for having let me go because only in that way could I learn the hard way and really understand my errors."

"At that point, I really understood that I didn't want the life that offered me the world. At the beginning, it seemed so great but at the end, it would just stab me in the back. Life with God isn't an easy life because every day we have to deal with people who think differently than we do, but I want to follow this way because it is the way of Eternal Life."

"Whosoever will have left houses, brothers, sisters, father, mother or fields because of my name, will receive one-hundred times over the same and at the end will inherit eternal life." (Matthew 19:29-30)

"So I want to invite each of you to not be ashamed of the Gospel because you can spread the Word to others who still have not understood the greatness of God."

"For I am not ashamed of the Gospel of Christ for it is the power of God unto salvation for everyone who believes, to the Jew first and also to the Greek; because in it is revealed the righteousness of God by faith unto faith as it is written, the just shall live by faith." (Romans 1:16-17)

CHAPTER THIRTY-SEVEN

The Church's Dream –
A Home of Our Own
2004

As the years went by, God continued to bless our church-planting ministry. For many years, our 950-square-foot facility was packed to the gills. During summer weather, we would open the glass doors and put chairs out in the piazza in front of our place. The Wednesday night before we left for furlough in 2000, I announced to our folk that I was going to trust the Lord for funds to help us buy a property of our own. The twenty-some folk there that night looked at me as if to ask, "What have you been smoking?" I then explained that I had seen a prime piece of property, and I was going to ask God for it.

In the eight months that we traveled in the States reporting to our supporting churches, I frequently mentioned the dilemma that was facing us as a church and asked God's people to pray about a one-time special gift for this project. Money started to slowly come in as many of our supporters got the vision of what could be accomplished if we had our own land and larger facilities.

In the time that we were gone, Jonathan pastored the church. He had come over on a two-year short-term ministry after having completed his college, seminary, and internship in Grand Rapids. The church was greatly blessed through his ministry, and at our return, we found a revitalized church with a vision to reach out to our neighborhood for the glory of God. A big part of this change was due to the efforts of a team from Jonathan's home church, the Calvary Baptist Church of Grand Rapids, Michigan.

I must say that prior to this point, it seemed that at the end of every furlough when we would return to Italy, we would find a church with many problems to resolve. This time, it was different. The church had actually grown! One of the keys was that prayer had become a priority in our weekly schedule of services. We actually had half of our Sunday morning group gathering for an evening totally dedicated to prayer. It made a difference. So many times, our traditional "Prayer Meetings" are actually twenty minutes of songs, twenty minutes of Bible Study, fifteen minutes of prayer requests, and five minutes of prayer. God answers prayer, and He is glorified when His people dedicate time to Him in prayer.

As we got back from furlough into the rigors of the ministry, we began looking in earnest for a new place to meet. The property that I had first seen and desperately wanted turned out to be a bad deal, and we abandoned those plans.

One of our criteria in buying a building, in addition to the location, was that we could declare the entire value and pay tax on the entire property. You would think that being honest would be normal, but in Italy, it is normal to try and cheat the government. We had decided that for our testimony, we would not compromise our standards for any property. This decision seemed to be an obstacle in buying anything in Italy. Cheating the government on taxes seems to be a way of life for many.

At one point in our search for a new property, we were nearly at the place of signing a contract when we mentioned that since we were Christians, we would of course plan on declaring the entire value of the property and paying the taxes on it. The owner replied, "Well, I am certainly not going to sell to you and lose money. The deal is off." We were disappointed at first because we were so desperate to move out of our tiny rented facilities! Every Sunday became a difficult effort to resolve our space problem. There were too many people in too little space! Looking back, however, we have thanked the Lord many times over for protecting us several times from buying the wrong place with the wrong set of standards! God could never have continued to bless our ministry at that point.

In August of 2002, I got a phone call from Tiziana, the real-estate agent who was helping us look for a place. This lady, with her husband, had visited our church several years earlier during some Carrara meetings and seemed to have a real respect for what we are doing, in spite of being very religiously Catholic. She told me of a place, just down the street from our home, built thirty years ago. By the way, it had been built by an acquaintance of ours when we first came to Italy. It had been built as a carpentry shop, but for many years, it has been rented as a consignment shop (still in business) and a sweater factory.

(Through the eyes of faith we saw a church's meeting place)

To explain how well it was built, on the hot August day when we walked into the building, it was cool and dry inside! That sold me right then. But what were they asking for the property? The building, in an excellent location on a new roundabout, had 4,500 square feet of floor space and came on a corner property of 27,000 square ft. It had an asking price of $500,000. We were overwhelmed by that figure, but we were sure that the Lord was going to give it to us, for His glory. All this while, the Lord was already providing about $8,000 a month for the support of our ongoing daily television ministry, La Bibbia Oggi, and the 24/7 operation of Radio Luce. It would be no problem for God!

When we went to speak with the owners, the elderly widow introduced me to her son who now handles her business. She asked him, "Don't you remember the Reverend? He came to the hospital and visited your dad just before he died." To tell you the truth, I had entirely forgotten that hospital visit some twenty-five years before. As we talked business, we mentioned right up front our decision to pay the taxes on the entire price. The owner was appalled to think that someone might not do that! He then gave us his non-negotiable price of $500,000! It took us over six month to have enough cash on hand (twenty per cent of the purchase price) as well as to find a bank that would finance the balance of the project for our small group of believers, none of whom could offer great financial guarantees to the bank. For several months, we visited bank upon bank, not trying to find the best deal, just trying to find the one who would trust us to give us the money!

One day as I was walking into the bank at San Sisto where I have had an account for over thirty years, I was stopped by the director. "What is this I hear that you are looking to other banks for a loan for your church?" I responded, "We are just trying to find the best deal possible to finance our building." "No!" He replied. "We want to be a part of this project. Look around all you want and show me the best deal you are offered and we will do better!" We shook hands, and I didn't look any other place. They did end up giving us nearly $400,000 dollars for 15 years at a fixed rate of 4.75%. That came just before the financial crisis that has been pushing loan rates higher and higher. Praise the Lord!

When we went to sign the contract, the seller kept the original price that he had quoted us months before. As we went before the notary, the government agent to collect the tax, he told us that we did not have to pay tax on the entire amount. We said, "No, we want to pay the tax on the entire amount." He was very surprised and asked us if we had the money to do that. "Sure," we replied and then proceeded to write a check for about $90,000!

(God's future answer to our step of faith)

CHAPTER THIRTY-EIGHT

Crossing Jordan
2008

In May of 2008, our son Jeremy and his wife Francesca left their employment and sold their home in Grand Rapids to return to Italy so that Francesca could finish her university studies here. One of the first things that Jeremy accomplished in our church was to challenge us to get out of our cramped rental space and move into our new church. It was foolish to pay rent and a mortgage! Even though we hadn't even begun the renovation project, we could at least save our rent money and apply that to the mortgage as we lived side-by-side with the work that would be done on the church. I don't know if we thought about how much work it would be to clean up the church each week for the worship time on Sunday, but we took the step.

The last Saturday of June, 2008, we moved everything out of the "old" church. It was a strange feeling to say goodbye to the tiny place that we had opened for services in June of 1976. It seemed so huge at that point, but lately, there wasn't room for anyone more, there was no more parking, and surely the eighteen families living in the building were tired of coming in to the church and asking someone to come out and move the car that had been parked in front of theirs in the tiny parking lot.

The emotions ran rampant that day as I thought of the years when our babies were the only ones in the church family, when I had to go there each Sunday morning to turn on the heat, when I had come back to the field in the middle of a church split and found the phone locked in my office and I didn't have a key, when I got cornered by some angry church members and after they didn't succeed in getting me angry while they had screamed at me for a half an hour, they cried out with disappointment, "He's winning again!"

Praise the Lord we moved out of that place! Too many memories! Thank you Jeremy for your vision in leading us to take that step and get us to cross-over into the promised land—and that it is!

CHAPTER THIRTY-NINE

A Soccer Ministry for the Baptist Church

Another very important contribution that Jeremy brought to our church was the burden to get a soccer ministry started. When I came to Italy, I knew so little about soccer that my kids wouldn't even let me play with them, but I decided that I would get involved. Over the years, we have seen many unsaved kids come out to play soccer with us and then come out for various church activities where they have heard the Gospel. Among the young men we have reached out to, there have been those who are unchurched, Roman Catholics, Muslim, and Hindu.

An annual soccer tournament has also been organized by our church for evangelical churches in Italy as an evangelistic outreach. Each of the church teams which participates is required to have at least a third of their team made up of unsaved players. An evangelistic service is held during which the Gospel is presented to those who attend.

CHAPTER FORTY

Thank God for a Stroke (Not of Luck)
That Brought Us an Italian Pastor
2009

In September of 2009, the Lord blessed me with four mini-strokes in a week. After the first two, I finally went to the emergency ward, and the last two I experienced while in the hospital under observation.

I was not able to speak and had already settled with the Lord that if I had to spend the rest of my life writing notes to communicate, I would do it with His help. As I read my Bible on that first morning in the hospital, I read of Paul's tearful farewell to the elders of the church of Ephesus in Acts 20. As I read of Paul saying goodbye to those believers for the last time, many of them his children in the faith, I cried out in my heart to God, "Please don't let this be the end of my story here at Perugia!"

Jonathan was home in the States on a short furlough, and the immediate challenge we faced was who would preach on Sunday?

Lucio and Cristina Stanisci and their three children had just returned from the States, having completed their theological studies at Master's Seminary. They had come back to Italy to begin a church in the Rome area. They happened to be free that following Sunday, and Lucio was very gracious to come and speak for us at San Sisto on a very short notice. They were living temporarily with Lucio's mom in Porchiano, a small town in southern Umbria, and it would mean a drive of nearly an hour and half each way, but they were glad to do it to help us out in this time of emergency.

After returning home from the hospital, I was able to begin attending the church services, too. What a joy to hear Lucio preach! I had known him since shortly after his conversion in the early nineties and had enjoyed several opportunities of ministry together with him at an evangelical camp and School of Christian Living in the mountains where several of our church and family had attended over the years. I knew of the great personal sacrifice that he had made to answer the call of God in his life and move his family to southern California to prepare for the Lord's work.

Now, I was listening to a very polished and theologically prepared Italian preacher rightly dividing the Word of truth in my pulpit! He was preaching just like I would have, but without the American accent! My first thought was, "What if the Lord would give us someone like Lucio to take our church to the next level?" It had always been our prayer, since starting the church back in 1976, that the Lord would give us a theologically prepared and polished Italian pastor. It seemed that we had faced a lot of criticism for having been the pastor for so long. We needed an Italian pastor, but where would he come from? In the years, several potential "Timothys" had come through the ranks but had not ended up being the "faithful men" to whom the ministry could be committed. With no effort of our own, through no merits that we could claim, God sent us Lucio and his family and he is now pastoring the church along with myself, Jonathan, Daniel and Massimo.

CHAPTER FORTY-ONE

The Thirtieth Anniversary of Radio Luce
2011

In August of 2010, the Lord provided for Daniel, Elizabeth, Cristina, and Elisa to leave the deputation trail behind and finally arrive in Italy as part of the Baptist Mid-Missions team. Not that they weren't already a part of the team. In the eight years since they had returned to the States for college, Daniel had continued his valuable work on the radio by means of the internet. On several occasions, it had been necessary to fly him back over to Italy to work out some of the technical problems that we encountered with the radio. On many occasions, he had given up precious hours of sleep in his already busy schedule of being a husband, dad, student, and employee in the IT department at BBC.

It was a relief for all of us over here to finally have him back. Many improvements in the studio of Radio Luce, as well as in the AV ministry of the local church, have already been made, and he is just getting started!

As we celebrated the thirty years of continuous broadcasting of Radio Luce, I spoke about a miracle that is still continuing after thirty years. The privilege of entering thousands of homes in central Italy and now in the entire world by means of internet is more than we could have ever dreamed or asked when we first switched on the transmitter on December 27, 1980.

Over the years, God has provided financially in a miraculous way through the sacrificial gifts of His people. He has provided technical assistance right when we needed it. We have never had an "in-house" technician, but in these thirty years, we have broadcasted 24/7 continuously with the exception of possibly a month of broadcast time. That is a miracle in itself.

Thousands of families have contacted us over the years, and many have visited our church. A number of them have actually been saved, baptized, and added to our local church and others. It has been worth all the sacrifice. It has been worth the investment of time. It was definitely worth it to see our children get involved and learn the joy of serving the Lord in this way.

When we began the station we were one of about thirty evangelical stations. Because of various problems, we are now one of about ten who are left.

God has been good to us.

(Radio Luce studio)

CHAPTER FORTY-TWO

His Story Is also the Future

As we look into the future, it is bright because we know the One who is holding it in His hand. With the Lord bringing all our children (and grandchildren) back to Italy to minister with Rachel and me, it just can't get much better than that until we are all with Him for eternity!

So many have asked us as missionary parents how we ever got all our kids to want to come back to Italy. Well, we didn't do it. It is certainly not because we were such excellent parents. My heart still aches for the time when I lost my patience with Josh and struck him. I still regret never taking time out of my busy church-planting, TV ministry, and radio ministry work load to take Jeremy fishing. By the way, the boys have forgiven me, but I still feel badly about it.

What can I say? As rough as things might have gotten, Rachel and I never considered quitting. God had put us here. "Occupy 'til I come" has rung in my spiritual ears many a time. We knew that God had called us to serve Him here, so there was no sense in complaining about the mission, our co-workers, or the Italians in front of our kids. We always considered our family to be a part of, not a hindrance to, the ministry. The blessings were not Dad's. They were all of ours as a family. The heartbreaks, however, were Dad's and Mom's. We didn't want to be responsible for our children growing up to hate God and resent what he had done in our family.

The toughest times were furloughs. We crammed into the car or van as much as possible. I needed my family with me to minister with me and make me look good! There were messages that the kids knew by heart and could have preached better than Dad in the case that he didn't feel well that Sunday. The "funnest" times were also furloughs. We got to do many special things as a family as we traveled. Several times, the kids got to go to Christian school, and they never had to go to school on Saturday like in Italy. The schoolwork in America was a piece of cake compared to what they were used to in Italy.

But that is the past. What about the future? God knows all of it; we know some of it. We know that God will be faithful, no matter what. We know that the gates of hell will not prevail against His Church. We know that this life will soon be past, but all that has been done for the glory of God will last forever.

We know that right now, we are enjoying life to the fullest as we serve God down here, but soon we'll be at the real party and we won't miss this one at all. I hope that you'll be with us on the other side.

Fred's Psalm

I taught a Bible survey class at our church's infant Bible institute and part of it was a study of the Psalms. To help the students understand them as an expression of David's faith and walk with God, I asked each of them to write a psalm of their own that would reflect their own experience with the Lord. Although we would never claim inspiration, our psalms were a great blessing to us all as we shared them in class. Here is mine. I trust that it will be a blessing to you too.

----

1. Oh God, you are my God. You chose me before you created the world.

2. You loved me while I was in my mother's womb, when I still had not heard your name.

3. You saved me while I was still a child, not having yet known all the depth of the wickedness of my heart.

4. In my adolescence you called me to your service while there was yet nothing that I could consider more important than total obedience to you with my life.

5. In my youth you preserved me from the evil that surrounded me by means of your Word that I studied and placed in my heart, thanks to the guidance of my parents.

6. In my marriage you blessed me, giving me a true help-meet, a companion in the work and an ecxcellent mother for my children.

7. In my parenthood you blessed me with children who would come to know you, who would serve you together with me, giving me great motives for joy and thanksgiving. All praise to you!

8. In my ministry you held me up, encouraged me and blessed me, even in the years of desert, when it seemed that the seed of your Word would not take root in the dry ground.

9. Even when I was under the attack of the enemy, with enemies without who wanted to devour me and the enemy within who wanted to destroy me, you were at my side, protecting me.

10. Now that I have hair tinted with silver and the blessing of seeing the children of my children I can repeat that you are my God, a Faithful God whom I want to worship for all eternity. Amen!

Finito di stampare nel mese di Giugno 2011
dalla Tipolitografia Grifo - Perugia